MY

AFRICAN

DREAM

Raising Visionary Leadership
For The Future of Africa

TONITO SAMUEL

For more information contact the author;
talktome@tonitosamuel.co.za

Book and Cover design by;
Bluebridge Technologies
Ignition Media.

Publisher
TMC-Publishing, A subsidiary of The Mind Coach
Johannesburg. South Africa

:

ISBN 978-0-620-59061-7

Before You Begin!

The content and concepts in this book are targeted towards three categories of people; to the first, this is an affirmation of what you already know. To the second category, this will quake and reposition your paradigm, and to the final group, it is absolutely a whole new scope of insight and perspective of reasoning. However, in whatever state or position you find yourself in, when you are done reading, I believe your perceptions, decisions, and judgments will no longer be fueled from a position of ignorance of governance or disconnect from politics and social responsibility. You are the one we've been waiting for.

Tribute

Will I have a complete judgment of Africa's past and present leaders who have in their own way made significant shift in governance and leadership without mentioning leaders such as Kwame Nkrumah of Ghana, Patrice Lumumba of the current Democratic Republic of Congo, Marion Ngouabi of the Congo Republic, Augostino Neto of Angola, Kenneth Kaunda of Zambia, Samora Machel of Mozambique, Amilcar Cabral of Guinea Bissau, Chief Obafemi Awolowo of Nigeria, whose vision gave free education to the western part of Nigeria, and Haile Selasie of Ethiopia with a view to acknowledge or say something about their local/national and all Africa role played by them? Certainly not.

I also wouldn't be fair on my tribute if I fail to mention a few of the many Jewish Anti-apartheid Activist such as; Joe Slovo, Helen Suzman, Sydney KENTRIDGE, I.A Maisels, Wolfie Kodesh, Albie Sachs who is currently serving as a member of the South African Constitutional court.

This is very important because some of them, especially Kwame Nkruma, Julius Nyerere, Kenneth Kaunda, Patrice Lumumba, Agostino Neto, Samora Machel, Amilcar Cabral,

Haile Selasie (the leader of Ethiopia, the only country which has been independent since time immemorial) are held in high esteem by most, if not all Africans on the continent and in the diaspora, for the leadership role they played.

My sincere appreciation goes to Ambassador Themba who indeed was instrumental to helping me focus on the great role these great African legends played and some still playing.

I am fully aware Nelson Mandela did not just miraculously emerge from outer space. He actually stepped into the footsteps of leaders who came before him, leaders who fought for independence and became the founding Presidents of their countries, leaders of countries that gave military training to Mandela and later offered similar training and refuge to South African guerrillas and refugees. By the time Mandela became South African President, he was already aware of the experience of other African countries and leaders, which he naturally could not ignore.

In the same vein, I celebrate many Africans and nations of Africa that has provided moral, diplomatic and material

iii

support to fellow African nations under the terrible economic, ethnic, religious and viral epidemic and tribulations. Thank you for being a Big Brother indeed.

I acknowledge Nigeria's role in providing academic opportunities to at least 300 South African exiles. I also wouldn't forget the struggle and sacrifice from Winnie Mandela, who almost single-handedly provided leadership to the black people of South Africa; she in her own way fought for what she believed.

Majority of these great leaders left a legacy, and one amongst all still stands out as my very best leader, for reasons best known to me. Nelson Mandela's leadership legacy has emerged as a world-class philosophy, he learnt from those he met in the struggle. What exactly is my generation learning from the present leaders? And what will the future generation learn from us?

Nelson Mandela
1918-2013
The Most
Influential Man on
the surface of the

I grew up longing to meet this great African and peacemaker, each time I stumbled on a material of his, I never hesitated in acquiring a copy. His principles and philosophies where the earth in the 21st Century very first thing that quaked my paradigm, I barely could come to term with how it is that a man could have what we Christians call the mind of Christ, a heart to forgive and let go of the hurt, deprivation, injustice and incarceration of 27 years, just for peace and the future of a nation.

Certainly, my interest and desire to meet a living legend grew stronger, unfortunately, I was only privileged to relocate to South Africa in 2013, at his very old age, and he was already sick, though I finally met him, but that was at his lying in state at the union building in Pretoria,

I still felt much fulfilled, as over 3 million people where gathered in one day to see this great man of our century. I remembered when I passed by his casket, I felt a strong wind, my logical conclusion of this experience can best be described as "that his spirit was very much around, smiling down on us, with a command, "carry on from where I stopped'. I probably would not be the only person on that ground that day who made a decision to make a difference. Tata's ordeal further proves that nothing good comes without a worthy price, nothing is indeed free, somebody somewhere and somehow has paid for it, or is paying for it, South Africans are indeed enjoying the benefits of peace drawn out of the lives of great men like Nelson Mandela, Walter Sisulu, Ahmed Kathrada, Raymond Mhlaba, Govan Mbeki, Elias Motsoaledi, Denis Goldberg and Andrew Mlangeni, O R Tambo.

Nelson Mandela, in whose legacy and ideals I represent and willfully dedicate my life in my own way and strategy to reignite the concept and ideals about true and visionary leadership driven by purpose for liberation, freedom, equality and nationalism.

A freedom fighter. An icon of selflessness, who in his own practice showed us how to love, forgive and be grateful. Who chose reconciliation in place of retribution. Who in his own words and action proved to us in Africa and the world at large that his struggle was not against white domination nor about black gaining domination but rather that all men, women and children irrespective of color or race deserves the right to be treated with equal respect without prejudice.

My African Dream is a cause Tata Madiba stood and fought for, with South Africa as a case study that love, forgiveness and gratitude are the best breeding ground for progress and prosperity of any nation.

COMMENDATION

"My African dream" This is more than a book. It's a diagnosis of the great sickness that Africa suffers from and a prescription for its cure - lack of visionary leadership. The time has come for the youth; the next generation of leaders of the African continent to turn the tide and become solutions to the problems that Africa is faced with. It all must begin with a dream; a vision; a new perspective of a new Africa. My African dream is a must have for all who desire to become leaders in any sphere of society; politics, business, entertainment etc. Congratulations once again Tonito you've indeed outdone yourself.

Wanda Mhobo
President Carpe Diem Africa Leadership Center

My African Dream sets out a crucial shift that is needed in the mindset of many people. Tonito Samuel is without doubt a great thinker on change. He convinces us that we can achieve our nation's dream and in the process teaches us how. I highly recommend this book for everyone regardless of your nationality.

Susan Okungbowa – Trainer,
CEO Trainwise Limited

Tonito Samuel's **My African Dream** *very appropriately identifies the challenges of leadership in Africa. His analytic take on the status quo is both visionary and pragmatic - advocating a "copy-cat" strategy to* *present some value based framework for developing African economies which are a global index for excellence. This book is essential reading for all Africans who aim to realise their full potential as leaders, global shapers, inventors and catalysts in a continent in dire need of them."*

Ndiana Matthew
Founder & CEO Palm3Strategy

DEDICATION

I dedicate this book to the Creator of heaven and earth, and the founder of the universe, who made me an African. And to every man and woman born to this continent as an African. Also to every person who has in time past advocated for change because they believed it was possible.

To those at the sideline probably complaining of the decay in the systems of government and leadership incapability. To the politician and public servants for daring to try and make a difference, and especially to the youths of my generation who has not given up hope and faith for a better leadership sprouting forth from the nations of this continent.

Also to you reading this book. You have taken the first step toward change, and I can only hope you become enlightened and equipped for the great task and responsibility ahead.

You are the most important, because as you learn, the eagerness to enlighten others will come upon you.

And finally, to the memory of Nelson Mandela, Tata, your struggles, success and philosophies have been one of my greatest inspirations for writing about Africa.

CONTENTS

FOREWORD

The request to write the forward came at a time when I was intensely preoccupied with the issues of life. Knowing Tonito for many years and being a man I had mentored and seen develop over the years meant saying no to him was out of the question. Our relationship, regardless, would not allow me break from my principled boundaries of only commenting on matters I have some knowledge over so writing a foreword without having read the book was therefore not even up for consideration.

Time nonetheless was of a great essence to the author and he had to make a hard choice, one I am today glad he did. The choice in question was a simple one, wait for me to create the time to read it or seek someone else with more time to write the foreword. On the day I began to read this book, I immediately understood why it was divinely positioned that it crossed my desk. Tonito poured of himself, as few are capable of, on a topic that resonates deeply with every son and daughter of Mother Africa.

He speaks, not as one without knowledge, but as a man of deep convictions, putting forward a very personal perspective of not just his dreams but also of his answers to building the Africa that so many of us know exists but are yet to experience.

His message speaks directly into the spirit and soul of his generation, with a voice that belies his age but is rather full of the wisdom that comes with the greyed hair of an elder. That in Madiba he found a worthy mentor is portrayed in every line one reads and it is only a worthy tribute to the great man, a true African and a firm believer in the enduring greatness of Africa's youth that he starts with him and closes on the very principles that made Madiba a living legend and an eternal hero; love, forgiveness and gratitude.

My African Dream is not the voice of one but the collective

voice of a generation. He speaks for an entire continent with words that many already are dying to say but don't have the gift to put across as articulately as he has. It is because of this gift I consider as priceless, I owe Tonito a lifetime of gratitude for if only those Africans in power today who claim to represent the people they lead, understand the virtues this book espouses and can decipher the message Tonito so passionately writes about, then the Africa, their Africa, our Africa no longer remains a dream but becomes our great and present reality.

Well-done Tonito.

Tonye P. Cole
Co-Founder Sahara-Group

_____*Second Foreword* _____

The ability to dream and envision the fulfilled manifestation of the dream as a reality is what dream releasers do. In his book, My African Dream, Tonito Samuel has systematically laid out his dream for a revitalized Africa. The ability to dream out loud and cause the dream to become a reality requires a level of commitment and sacrifice that few are willing to make.

It's the process of denying one's self in order to foster a better today for a people, a nation, and the world. Mr. Samuel has dared to dream out loud and release his concern for his country and countrymen at all expense.

This book is life altering, and will challenge you to step outside your comfort zone in order to help you gain an understanding of the severity of the situation in the continent of Africa. As you survey its content and navigate through the chapters, you will undoubtedly be faced with defining moments that will challenge you to make critical decisions and choices that will impact you, and set the course for the remainder of your life.

Every situation that the leadership of the great Continent of Africa is facing is a defining moment that's designed to elevate the people and Africa herself to a higher dimension of her value and purpose. When the minds of the people are elevated, Africa will be elevated because the people are Africa. Tonito has issued a challenge to the leadership of the Continent of Africa, to rise to the occasion and serve the people.

In essence, Mr. Samuel's dream is to see a transformed people and Africa by the renewing of the mind. Transformation is the key to a revitalized Africa. Until there is authentic internal transformation that's based upon the revelation revealed throughout these pages, we will not witness the external manifestation of the fulfillment of the dream. I challenge anyone that reads this book to ask himself/herself, what am I doing to make the dream become a reality? The power of transformation is the awakening of one's aware as they uncover and discover the wealth and value that's already contained within.

You are full of greatness. Africa and the world is waiting for you to come forth as the manifested dream that's written about within these pages. It's time to give birth to the dream, are you willing to endure the discomfort and pain of transformation in order to foster the transformation of a people and the world?

That is what Tonito has done and continues to do as he undergoes the birthing pains of giving birth to his dream of seeing a transformed people and Africa. Transformation takes place based upon what you consume. Be Empowered and Transformed.

Dr. Larry Carnes, Master Transformational
Leadership Life Coach, and Author of The Law of Servanthood,
www.larrycarnesministries.org

INTRODUCTION

I am one of those children who grew up asking a lot of questions, the "why nature" has always been part of what landed me into a lot of trouble while growing up. I have cared less sometimes about what happens around and what people do, rather I have learnt to concern myself with "Why it happened, why it is happening, they call it curiosity, but I think it is hunger for change that has driven me into the good, bad and ugly side of every event of life.

Experience has proven beyond reasonable doubt that transforming a system does not require rocket science, for every change, a process of purpose driven action deliberately marshaled is required to produce expected or desired result. Why is this credence so strong in my idea? It is because; never in reality has anyone, without a plan for change or transformation woken up to see that the changes have brought themselves without him/her playing a role. One of my best laws of life is Newton's Laws of motion, especially the first and the third law, the initial, which is generally referred to as the law of the inertia states that

"Every object in a state of uniform motion tends to remain in that state of motion unless an external force is applied to it. My interpretation of this law is simply, "nothing works unless you make it work, nothing changes unless you decide to change it, no difference will be made unless somebody decides to make a difference.

This simply means that to make a difference, action is required, you and I must learn to imbibe the principle and practices that govern the law of making a difference; now the world has become too advanced for any society to be lay-back. Whatever the change we may be trying to invent and implement, somebody somewhere, may have already implemented them; rather we should embrace the culture of finding what works and working on it, "borrow the wheel" is the principle the world on the fast lane is adopting to keep up with the pace of changes. My African dream is simply my perspective and version of a new continent, with a generation of people renewed in their thinking. A people completely transformed through enlightenment and also equipped with noble character. A people willing to lay down best moral, spiritual and ethical principles that will govern the states and help prepare the foundation of trans-generational development in all spheres of life.

My African dream is to behold a people bound by one purpose, one dream, one hope and one voice. A people who seeks for the advancement of others than self, a continent void of classism, racism and terrorism, a continent where love, tolerance and mutual respect are the foundation and pillars holding our diversities together. For only with these mindsets can we raise a vision driven continent.

This handbook is my ideology drawn from my personal opinion, followed by observation from the happening around my society. It is 100% purpose-driven, core centered on leadership and systems of governance practiced in Africa and how best we can employ and enjoy true democracy. Reading through, you will understand my paradigms and motives behind the craving for a vision and purpose driven system of governance, which, if considered for adoption can be the catalyst for our dream continent.

Then only will the possibility of a generation with transformed thinking hungry for change be easily integrated into our contemptuous, crooked classification of governance and visionless leadership to enforce change in a positive dimension. In any educational institution, to copy during an examination or test is malpractice. I remember, once you are caught spying, you are automatically labeled a *"Copy Cat"* the word copy-cat today has a totally different meaning to me, simply because I am inspecting from another lens from which I am able to see better and engage more benefit of copying to success, in the corporate world of today, what we regard as competition is born out of the act of copying, to copy is accepted and very much encouraged and it is actually the fastest way to get results if the sources and objectives are right.

There is this common saying, – *why re-invent the wheel*? If you need a wheel, just find one who has a wheel and borrow it. My greatest mentor and teacher, Jesus Christ, the savior of the world even taught some sense in this light. He had a need for a donkey, he could have used his creative power to create one, but he sent his disciples to go to the city and that they would find a donkey tied down, he commanded them to untie it and bring it for the occasion.

China grew her economy from one of the poorest economies in world history to the biggest and largest economy in the world of today. China, regarded in time past as poor and third world, is now salvaging and supporting other one

xxii

time great economies from collapse. The big question the world should be asking the likes of China, United Arab Emirates, India, Indonesia, Malaysia is, *"How did you guys do it?"*

These nations transformed from what and who they were economically, socially and of course, mentally, to what they have today and who they have become by the act of probably *"Copying"* the world best economy and they got even better result. A very intelligent mind would rather ask, *"What exactly should we copy? Is it culture? System? Structure or what?*

This book is going to address an enviable and positive-covetous approach to success in our personal life and a democratic system as a nation and a continent. Our ability to lead in this area of life will produce for us the dream continent or nation we all desire. Every 17th of August, we celebrate the life of a living legend, the sacrifice he and his colleagues made was all a price for the dream South Africa.

If we can think it, we can achieve it,

If we can dream it, then it's absolutely possible,

If we can conceive it, we can create it.

And if we can indeed create it, we can have it in reality.

Dream is what is required to transform a nation;

Your dream today is the reality of your tomorrow.

For this to be real as we see it in our imagination,

We must find what works and work on it.

MY AFRICAN DREAM

The Root Problem

At the commencement of this book, I was absolutely convinced that copying the works and patterns of successful people can equally make you successful. I know and understand better today that you can copy what people do, and never have a clue as to why they do it. This further explains that purpose is key to anything we do or want to do. In order to provide a lasting solution for our Africa, the real root cause must be addressed, and from my point of view, "Visionlessness and Lack of Purpose".

These are the root problems ravaging the system of governance in Africa; if there are things worth combating and tackling, it is these two trans-generational epidemics. As little a problem they may sound, as we go deeper in this chapter, you will be amazed to see the magnitude of negative effect the absence of this virtue has on us. Before I begin to rail out the numerous disadvantages from lack of vision in our personal life and nations, I would want us to be clear as to what vision, being a leader and visionary leadership are about.

Also, I crave your indulgence to understand why we will dwell so much talking about vision and purpose in this chapter, because, it is the absence of it that has broken down our walls of patriotism, integrity and social responsibility. I believe once we get it right from the foundational perspective, then laying the bricks of development becomes far more easy than imagined, repositioning and transformations becomes attainable and very much sustainable.

What is vision?

A **vision** is a revelation about the future of a person, people or group that is giving by God alone to the visionary, and it is only seen with the mind.

The greatest gift given to humankind is not the gift of sight, but the gift of vision, why? Because sight is a function of the eye while vision is a function of the mind.

For sight is an enemy to vision because, Sight is limited to the capacity of your eyes, while vision is limited only to the boundaries of your imagination.

Sight restricts you to the present. But Vision releases you to the unchartered frontiers of the future.

Vision is the capacity to see farther than your eyes can look, these are the greatest characteristics lacking in our society. Leadership requires that you see beyond your eyes, it is also the impact of the pursuit of your vision that is nobler than your self-preservation

The source of vision is inspiration

The source of inspiration is passion

The source of passion is purpose

3

The source of purpose is divine impartation

The source of divine impartation is your reason for creation

Dr. Myles Munroe

What is Leadership?

Leadership is the power of influence through character impact.

From this definition, it's clear a leader has the capability to *"influence"*, and a leaders greatest medium of influence is his/her *"character"*, this further implies that your character is who you are, and who you are is seen through what you do and how you do them.

This is my own definition of who a leader is: A leader is someone who looks ahead (visionary) into the future, envisages the trouble of the future, and begins now (today) to create possible solutions to tackle tomorrow's problem.

Don't let it be a surprise; vision may sound relatively ambiguous or unfamiliar to so many political leaders of today!

Leadership is a concept established on moral principles that demands complete sacrifice of one's pleasure for others to benefit first.

A leader **thinks first** about the benefits of the people he serves. *A true leader only sees himself as an arrowhead, but still a part of the arrow.* A good leader listens, learns and shares other people's opinion that are in accordance with the core and fundamental moral principles that produces the reality of the vision or dream required to deliver good and effective governance for the system.

For leadership is based on inspiration, not domination; on cooperation, not intimidation.

In a democratic system, the people decide who should lead them based on what they see and think, a true leader thinks of all possible ways to exceed the expectations of the people he is serving. *Leadership is service* and not dictatorship as the case is in some countries in Africa. A leader who lacks foresight can be likened to a physically sightless (blind)

5

person. Imagine the challenges, disadvantages and limitations facing such a person? This illustration will help us a long way in understanding the degree of limitation we are faced with as a people or nation without vision.

Comparing Lack of Sight to Lack of Vision

The lack of vision is the inability to have a mental picture of a preferred future, as earlier illustrated, the lack of vision can be likened to a physically challenged person, and these are the limitations encumbering such a person.

Environment Interaction

Blind people can have difficulty interacting with their environment, it can become difficult to perceive where one is and to get from one place to another, and movement can become restricted, leading to having little contact with the surrounding world.

Social Interaction

Blind people are often restricted in their ability to interact socially. There can be an apprehension or awkwardness on the part of sighted people when dealing with the blind, which can lead to difficulty for the blind in developing relationships. As a result, they are often relegated to specific roles in society and are usually held to lower standards and expectations.

Visual Symbols

Much of how we communicate is through the use of visual symbols. We depend on what we see to warn us of danger, to provide direction and to interact with people. The blind person is often placed in a situation of being excluded from these symbols, which in effect cuts them off from a portion of the world. This aspect explains my concept of leadership or who a leader is, through signs and events, a leader can foresee and foretell, sometimes it's called discernment, but it all boils down to one common attribute, "Vision".

7

Public Perception

The blind have to deal with a public perception that they are not capable of functioning effectively in society as sighted people. According to the National Federation of the Blind, the visually impaired face a form of prejudice that can hold them back, and can only be eliminated through continuous efforts to educate the public. Interestingly, the same issues that people who are physically impaired faces are the same those who lack inner vision are facing.

Sight and vision are two different things, vision is the eyes of the mind, vision can be termed as revelation, dream, insight, purpose, I can also call it eyes of understanding, the fundamental truth is clearly stated in the book of wisdom, Proverbs 29:18 says *"Where there is no vision, the people perish"*.

Analyzing the disadvantages of lack of vision to that of the physically impaired, as it relates to our personal and national life, we will affirm that the effects are similar and even higher in terms of its ripple effect.

Research has shown that well over 80% of African's today seek to become citizens of well focused and purpose driven countries, especially western countries, why? Because they want to be associated with greatness and good name; these two major defects are killing the pride of Africa, and it's not paving a way for the future as the average African Child grows up to be inferior mentally and emotionally to the average western child, reasons being that the average American or western child has a full understanding of what it means to be an American or Westerner, he or she is born and nurtured as a first class citizen of the world.

Lack of a Leader

I sincerely believe our major root cause is the lack of visionary leaders. A political position does not imply you are a leader, that you are a manager in a very reputable organization still does not qualify you as a good leader, leadership is an act, meaning it can be learned or acquired, but a few find the traits of leadership within and go the extra mile to develop it. This session draws our attention to what the society and system loses when true and visionary leadership is misplaced: I'll recommend any of John Maxwell's books on leadership. It's needful to emphasize more on **who and what makes a great leader**.

Visionless Leadership

We have been plagued for too long a time with this cancerous epidemic. I believe it is trans-generational and the biggest killer of the ability to create. Visionless leadership is a fundamental issue, and when not addressed, no matter how much we patch the structure, with time, it will collapse. My quest for why things are happening around the politics and governance in our society drove me to ask one key question, which is; *what basis was independence and liberation from colonialism founded upon?* Was it based on the foreseen future of building a better life for the country or was it just a private ambition? I take a cue from one of the greatest legends, Nelson Mandela and his crew who fought for freedom In South Africa, a struggle that was founded upon a vision of building a multiracial nation where all will be equal. Unfortunately, I cannot tell you exactly the reason(s) why Nigerian founding fathers fought for independence, but I can tell you, it was not visionary, it was not futuristic and neither was it meant for the generation which I now live in, because if it was, 54 years is very much enough for the essence of the freedom and independence to begin to surface.

Visionary leadership is the ability to cause other people to see a vision of the future that is bigger than their private ambitions; no nations in Africa will come out of obscurity and poverty if the private ambitions of the supposed leaders are conflicting with a national objective. Leadership is a capacity to make a vision everybody's vision, that's why larger percentages of political leaders can't make any significant impact in their community, because they are so consumed with their private interest and not interest in the next generation. A leadership drenched with vision embarks on development that he may never benefit from, but the generation yet unborn some hundreds years in the future will live, forever grateful.

So therefore, visionless leadership is simply the inability for a leader to see into the future. This is where Africa as a whole is as at today. I personally appreciate just one country in Africa, and that's South Africa, they are not there yet, but a good foundation has been laid, but it is quite easy to destroy if private ambition overrides public interest as the case is gradually emerging today in the politics of South Africa. We have 57 countries in Africa, and I seriously doubt it, if 50% of these nations have a clue of who they are, why they exist, for what purpose they as a nation and a people has come to fulfill.

It is, and will always be the role of the leader to point people to a direction of purpose, unless we find that leader in us, we may never be able to combat corruption.

Drivers, Not Drivels

It will be of great importance to know that there is a huge contrast between dreamers and blabbers, vision and action-less voices, drivers and drivels, in relations to the purpose of the enlightenment, I desire readers to grasp *the term blabbers or drivels, as this will be used to represent mere and empty speeches, motionless motivations and unfulfilled promises.*

True vision is progressive, it has its beginning and never ends, because it's ever evolving, innovatively meeting the needs of the present, removing the barriers and reinventing the future, just to make sure errors of the past are completely eradicated.

In my first book 2030, I dedicated a chapter to explaining

various dimensions that are required before we can call life a success, to dream is just the foundation, making that dream a reality requires so many angles and dimensions. I believe you are well aware that laying a building's foundation does not actually mean the house will be built.

Likewise, to have a dream is likened to the foundation of a building, to dream is not enough, because if dreaming alone was all that men required to succeed in life, then all men would be billionaires. In the dimensions of success, I mentioned five key dimensions that must be attained in order to bring you to a realm of success.

Between your dream and reality, there are pathways, plans, strategy, processes, time, people, places, events which will mold and define the attitudes that will determine if indeed you are heading the right direction towards success or not. Again, I throw this question to you, what do you understand by the word dream?

A 'dream' is a seed that has the capacity of producing a mighty forest large enough to serve the whole world, if only sown on the right soil and nurtured from time to time.

Another definition says a dream is *a clear mental picture of a preferred future given by God, based on an accurate understanding of God, self and circumstances.*

If I'm to analyze this definition, you will discover it has three components, which are:

- ✓ A source
- ✓ A conveyor
- ✓ A destination

The source of every dream is God.

According to Dr. Myles Munroe:

The source of vision is inspiration

The source of inspiration is passion

The source of passion is purpose

The source of purpose is divine impartation

The source of divine impartation is your reason for creation

The conveyor is you; the one who has caught a glimpse of the future is called the seer. The conveyor is also the mind of whom the vision appears or is revealed to. He or she is the carrier of the vision, wherever he/she goes, there goes the vision.

A destination is purpose in the context of our discussion. Dreams are meant to meet a particular need or intent that will leave lasting impact even after we are gone. From our understanding about the source of a dream or vision, it is clear we are all here on earth for a reason.

Now my greatest worry on earth is that many times some individuals endeavor to know why they exist, but never live for that reason. While the vast majority really does not have a clue as to why they exist. If nothing else catches your attention from this book, remember and keep this to heart that *the greatest discovery in life is destiny and you must find yours.*

How many nations have ever asked why they became a

republic, or a federation or a nation? The reality is that, many countries just like ours in Africa can be likened to an individual who does not know who he is. If I may ask, Why are we a republic?

There is one great country in the world that I love with all my heart. The United States of America, this nation thinks, believes, lives as *'Voltron', the defender of the universe.* America believes the world deserves freedom and liberty, and they go all the way to show the world how much understanding they have about their role to the rest of the nations of the earth. This is a clear sign of a nation who knows and understands purpose.

A dream born out of intent of existence will do one great thing in your life, which is; *Change the lives of people around you*, because the real beneficiaries of that dream is not you, it's not even your family, but it is for a people, a nation, a continent or even the world. You are a conveyor, and your family will reap the benefits of a successful conveyor.

Dreams come true, but only through a process of time, for your dreams to be realized, you have to conform to certain principles and qualities, one of them is complete self-denial, this is an extreme sacrificial state, where born leaders put the cause ahead of self.

Self-Denial

This is a state of the denial of one's own interests and needs; self-sacrifice, dreamers unconsciously enter into this state. A true leader is dead to his personal needs. He seeks for the good of others. Let me startle your mind a little bit. Do you think Nelson Mandela and the other freedom fighters of South Africa were not given the option to forget about the struggles and fight against apartheid, to take some good life offers and live a happy life for themselves?

But for purpose of the struggle, which was to have a South Africa where equality and freedom was a fundamental human right. That struggle gave birth to the South Africans living today in peace. That was a dream come true. Surprisingly, Nelson Mandela became president and after four years, he handed over power, peacefully, he didn't see power as a compensation for the fight for freedom he spent most of his youthful life pursuing, he gave it up.

While in other countries in Africa, people who have not sacrificed anything for the country, people who by time and chance got themselves into power have made the seat of power theirs and children's birthrights and inheritance. Such people are drivels.

Drivers are result oriented and pragmatic.

Action is the vital part of a dream; there is a saying, "where there is a will, there is a way", *'Drive' comes as a result of the acceptance of the dream, which is the willingness to make your dream a reality.*

The will to act or do propels actions. It is the point or time phase that measures the level or amount of faith/believe in that dream.

20

Drive is simply giving your faith a foot. No matter how beautiful the promise land is, you still will have to go and possess it. Without drive we won't achieve anything in life. 'Drive' like I said, is the energy we bring to the realization of our dreams. It is the force that we exert to making sure that our dreams come true, it is those sleepless nights, the searching for means to make them work and getting them to reality.

Another word for drive is passion. This continent needs drivers. Men and women passionate about bringing change and pride back to this continent. People to lead us to the promise land. Leaders who will take bold initiatives and giants gaits to drive the change we all desire.

To administer change in a decaying society such as ours is no mere or cheap political talk.

Who is a driver?

The dictionary defines a driver to be:

1. A person who drives a vehicle: a taxi driver | student drivers

2. A factor that causes a particular phenomenon to happen or develop

But my simple definition is that a driver is someone who leads, by taking or moving people from one point to another based on his or her higher knowledge and understanding called revelation or experience of the supposed destination.

Leaders or drivers are those who go the extra mile to see that all that was promised to the masses during a political campaign and manifesto is carried out to the letter.

Below, we are going to share some insightful qualities of a good driver/leader. These qualities as expected in a vehicle driver, is equally a requirement expected from a good leader driving a system to its next destination.

Qualities of a good driver

- Knowledge
- Skill

- Self-Discipline

- Concentration

- Anticipation

- Attitude

Knowledge

Knowledge is facts, information, and skills acquired by a person through experience or education. Knowledge is awareness, acquaintances, gen, expertise, familiarity; it is the theoretical or practical understanding of a subject, and the subject matter today is leadership.

Knowledge is one of the most important qualities of a good driver or leader. I have come to understand that the major reason why our nations are suffering from politicians who claim to be leaders is simply because the supposed leader really does not know what it takes to be a leader. Politicians from all indications have proven to us, that they lack the concept and understanding of leadership. When you employ a chauffeur to drive you for the first time, all you want to do is to ascertain his knowledge and understanding on driving and traffic rules, based on this knowledge you can then decide if he is good for the keep or should be let loose. Africans must come to the state of ascertaining the level of knowledge, understanding and expertise on leadership before casting votes or throwing supports for any political office runner.

Skill

This quality is higher than knowledge, because skill is applicable in critical situation or scenarios, the way and manner a driver handles the steering, overtakes on the road, controls speed, escapes pot-holes, drives during traffic jams tells how much skill born out of experience that driver has in his prowess, so it is for a leader. Leadership skills are made visible *when the citizens or people you lead can measure your decision-making abilities, measure how you manage pressure,*

24

and measure how you flow when things don't seem to turn out the way you planned or envisaged.

Self-Discipline

A good driver has self-control, he knows how to puts his will under control, his opinions matters less as long as his boss has an opinion, he is so disciplined to the point he knows when to restrain. These attributes are of great and immense benefit to a nation if it's leaders possesses them. One of the ways to measure self-discipline is the ability to not abuse privilege and power bestowed on you as a leader by the people.

Here in Africa, especially my country Nigeria, a police officer with a grade 12 certificates and no further training, addresses anybody with contempt. In few countries of the world that I have had the privilege of travelling to, I enjoy interacting with the police, because they have an attitude that makes them approachable.

25

I must emphasize, you do not require a title to be conferred on you before you become a leader. In whatever position of responsibility or service you find yourself, these qualities ought to be prevalent in you.

Concentration

A good driver or leader has huge attentiveness and unshaken concentration on where he is going to and much more on how to get there. The greatest distraction to a driver and anybody heading somewhere important in life is the loss of focus. To concentrate means to stay focused.

So many nations in Africa today have lost concentration on the realities of the present day. From my own viewpoint, I believe my country Nigeria is one of those nations that has lost focus. Once concentration is lacking, every distraction possess itself as an attraction. Have you ever seen nations, political office holder's debate over senseless issues?

The parliaments, upper house or lower house as the case may be, deliberating over matters that will not move the nation an inch towards success, those are signs of a distracted government.

Anticipation

A good driver has an expectation to reach his destination; so all eagerness or anticipation is focused on the final destination. When we board airbuses and it's about to take off, the pilot announces the estimated time of flight and time of arrival, which becomes the expectation of the passengers and that of the pilot. Because a good driver knows first where he is going, he is so focused, yet he is so hopeful to get to his final destination in peace.

Every leader who cannot give or build the expectations of his people is not a good leader.

Attitude

This quality is the greatest of them all, why do I say so? The other qualities mentioned can actually earn you the job, but what will guarantee job sustainability is called 'Attitude'. Always remember, you will be hired for what you know, but can be fired for who you are, your attitude is who you are. For it is the settled way of your thinking or feeling about someone or something, typically one that is reflected in your behavior.

From this definition, it is clear that attitude is a total reflection or interpretation of a thinking pattern or behavior of a person, attitude affects all you do and can tell how far a person can go in life. For attitude is the most substantial qualities a driver needs to drive the vehicle of life, or purpose of a mission to it's realistic or desired destination.

The right attitude attracts right people, and the right attitude reshapes the mindset of people around you and turns them around for your favor. The right attitude will always repel negative people who do not want change. The right attitude automatically creates an environment that provides opportunity, right attitude enables the thinking ability capable of birthing change in any circumstances or environment, a person or driver with the right attitude is quick to listen and learn, a person with the right attitude is always willing to help, nurture and mentor anyone willing to learn.

The Drivels

A drivel only talks and does not have the drive to implement, sometimes I get to think most politicians in Africa are drivels. I have observed from the manifestos of political parties, to presidential speeches of various countries in comparison to the kind of energy and hunger for change expected, I personally see nothing. I remember standing and gazing at my TV, when President Obama was first sworn in as president of the United State. From his speech, you could tell this man had something to offer, same thing happened when he won his second term in office. A more matured and experienced Obama spoke even more and deeper purpose.

I cannot remember the presidential speeches of any president that has ruled my country Nigeria, simply because the speeches were probably not worth remembering or remarkable. If we go searching for those speeches, they may have said something very meaningful and remarkable, but one major reason why you and I may find it difficult remembering is because they probably were not backed with action.

Have you ever wondered why politicians from Africa take the citizens for a ride? Quite a majority of the political parties in Africa are a bunch of drivel, what ideology do each party actually represents and stands for? What's the philosophy of each of the political parties in your country? Any idea? Interestingly, I have tried checking out the website of the major political parties in my country, PDP and Action Congress. Frankly speaking, I seriously cannot tell the philosophies of these parties.

The manifestos and objectives I found on the Action Congress website appeared more to me like a project tabloid, which brings me back to the place of worry. How can the common man relate to the outlined project based manifesto on the ACN website? Nonetheless, the same party has been the only group who has made a significant impact in the states they are ruling.

The common man can relate to their work, because it is visible, the common man can easily associate with the brand and prospects of the Action Congress Party, why? Because works don't lie, these may not be said affirmatively for other political parties in Nigeria, I do not belong to any political party, so let no one think I am promoting ACN and discrediting others. Please find manifesto of the ACN on this link below. http://actioncongressnigeria.org/manifesto/ And you can find that of PDP the ruling party from this link below. http://peoplesdemocraticparty.com.ng/?page_id=72 .

Comparing the manifesto of ACN and PDP's manifesto with that of The Republican party of the United States, I found out that the manifesto is centered on value and beliefs, and not a task or proposed projects and objectives. People connect easily to a cause only when they see that cause aligning with their beliefs.

So a manifesto should connect to people. When we set up organizational structures, part of the most important ethics we make sure is driven down to the very last employee is the company's Core Value. It's about what the organization believes and doesn't believe. It's about the perception and paradigm of the organization, hence, the understanding is the culture built in the working environment, that culture is what is transferred to clients and customers, that culture is what generates the revenue for the organization, same lies with a vision driven political party, the value or manifesto has to be tailored towards character building. Below is an excerpt of the manifesto of the Republican Party in the United States.

ABORTION

The platform recognizes that "the unborn child has a fundamental individual right to life which cannot be infringed," thus opposing abortion in any circumstances. It opposes government support for organizations that perform or advocate abortions.

IMMIGRATION

The platform calls for the federal government to abandon lawsuits against states that have introduced tough anti-immigration laws such as Arizona and Alabama and opposes any amnesty for illegal immigrants or their children. It advocates making English the national language.

33

GUNS

The GOP has not been moved to restrict the sale of guns or ammunition by the recent mass shootings. "We oppose legislation that is intended to restrict our Second Amendment rights by limiting the capacity of clips or magazines or otherwise restoring the ill-considered Clinton gun ban."

MARRIAGE

The platform backs a constitutional amendment defining marriage as the union of one man and one woman and affirms the rights of states not to recognize gay marriage. It condemns the persecution of traditional marriage advocates by hate groups that support gay marriage: "We condemn the hate campaigns, threats of violence, and vandalism by proponents of same-sex marriage against advocates of traditional marriage and call for a federal investigation into attempts to deny religious believers their civil rights."

TAXATION

"We reject the use of taxation to redistribute income, fund unnecessary or ineffective programs or foster the crony capitalism that corrupts both politicians and corporations."

HEALTHCARE

The party supports the immediate abolition of Obama-care and the conversion of the limited public health insurance that exists for the elderly and poor into a voucher system.

INTERNET

The party has extended its defense of the protection of individual rights to include digital data. "We will ensure that personal data receives full constitutional protection from government overreach and that individuals retain the right to control the use of their data by third parties; the only way to safeguard or improve these systems is through the private sector."

Read   more: http://www.smh.com.au/federal-politics/blogs/altered-

states/after-the-storm-republicans-quietly-release-manifesto-20120830-
2527w.html#ixzz354v33RgN

Reading through the contents on this website gave me a clue of what the Republican Party believes and stands for, this is what manifesto means. What I see in Nigeria are too ambiguous and reading through that of the ruling party, I still couldn't find my bearing on exactly what the party stands for from the manifesto.

Affirmatively, there are millions of people who share my view as to not knowing the core objectives and purpose of the existing political parties in Nigeria, even so, it is for so many countries in Africa, parties spring up here and there and the question is why?

I had initially thought that Africans are politically passive. I had concluded that my generation and those younger are not keen about politics, but that line of thought is actually not completely true, we may not be interested in the day to day processes, but we know what change is, and if there is anything we want to see happen is 'Change'.

This generation is tired of visionless politicians who don't have a clue as to where we are going as a nation, needless to drive us there, we are fed up of having rogues, liars, thieves celebrated as politicians. If the president can tell the world that stealing is ordinary and not corruption, then we are in a deep hot soup of destruction, I believe in this entity called Nigeria, and would not want to see it crumble completely in the hands of visionless leaders.

We are tired of being abused emotionally, psychologically, economically and intellectually. We seek for only one thing, true men and women with integrity who are willing to drive us towards change and help us build a future for the people of our nation and the continent; we are seeking for drivers and not drivel.

Who Will Dream For Us?

3

After numerous observations and research on thriving economies and countries with great and meaningful impact on the surface of the earth today, two things were eminent and common, 'a dream' and 'a dreamer'. I learnt from one of my greatest mentors, Stephen Corvey, *that an organization is a lengthened version of one person dream or vision.*

Meaning, the fortune 500 companies we celebrate today actually are an idea which sprung up from the mind of just one person, and that one person, strategically, systematically, planned, pursued and planted the vision into the minds of his/her team and a singular vision, became an organizational or collective vision.

The book of wisdom says, one will chase a thousand, and two will chase ten thousand. For every idea and successful business standing today, there is a man or woman who is the conveyor. When you think Microsoft, you think Bill Gates, when you think Apple, you think Steve Jobs. When you think light bulbs, you think Thomas Edison, and when you think of telephone, you will think of Alexandra Graham Bell and Antonio Meucci. When you think mobile telephone, you will think of Martin Cooper, and when you think internet, you will think of Tim Banners Lee, when you think of Facebook, you will think of Mark Zuckerberg, when you think of salvation, you will think of Jesus Christ just to mention a few.

Narrowing this thought process towards national legacy and nation building, when you think of The United States, who comes to mind? Benjamin Franklin, George Washington and Abraham Lincoln. When you think of South Africa, Nelson Mandela comes to mind. When you think of Dubai, HH Sheikh Mohammed comes to mind. Ideas are spirit, and they will always require bodies and minds to embody them. This chapter is centered on the impacts and legacies, founding fathers, revolutionists, visionary and purpose driven ideals handed down generations, and comparing them with what our own founding fathers left behind, if they left any.

If they didn't develop a compass to navigate our paths and find meaning as a nation, then who will dream for us?
The amazing and uncovered revelation about life is that "Vision is the greatest inheritance a father can offer or pass down to his children and unborn generation"

This thesis begins my reasoning, it is the role of the fathers to dream, the book of wisdom says:
' On the last days, God said, for I will pour out my Spirit upon all flesh, your Sons and Daughters shall prophesy, your young men shall see 'Vision' your old men shall 'Dream Dreams '…

40

From this text above, it is clear that 'dreams are meant to be caught by Old Men and young men see vision. Deeper understanding is required here, because the young man reading this book will be old someday. I believe it's the obligations of fathers to dream and create a pathway for their children, because dreams and visions almost mean the same thing. It's important to know that dreams come as a result of signs of warnings, guidance or revelation, and the same with vision, some school of thought says dreams come to you while you are asleep, while vision comes to you while you are awake.

It's so clear that the vision and dream for national transformation will have to start from the mind of somebody, someone who will be bold enough to sacrifice all for the reality of this dream and for the people. Someone fearless, focused, driven by inner conviction and purpose. Someone who knows and understands that one of his or her reasons for living is to fulfill this one cause, which is to see that this vision or dream becomes a reality. Nelson Mandela and the crew sacrificed 27 years of their life in jail, excluding the numbers of years of public cry and molestation from a mentally derailed racist minority. They endured the pain for the gain of all. Who said they were not offered the easy way out, who said they never had a second thought, who said they never felt betrayed even by the people they were fighting for at some point, but they took all the humiliation just for the unity and justice and a peace loving South Africa of today.

African nations are earnestly awaiting the dreamers or visionary leaders who will lead us out of the obscure bondage of self-inflated-poverty ravaging our nations.

Life is completely founded upon fundamental principles and laws, as long as we never dream for anything; we also get nothing in return.

The change and transformation we seek is locked up inside the mind of somebody and that person has got to let it out.

That person could be you. I have read articles from some blogs about various countries in Africa, and the outcry and outburst is just the same. From Angola to Zimbabwe, the cry is similar, resulting from visionless leadership.

In order to get clear answers for this context, every person yearning for a political position should do so with a master plan of a vision that will transform the nation from its deadened states. The deliverance of your country lies in your hands. You as a citizen have the key to unlock the doors of greatness and usher your nation and the generation yet unborn into a lifetime of purpose and pride.

It may appear unrealistic and unachievable especially when you have to consider your background or pedigree that you do not in any way qualify to make a difference, but that is a myth. You must believe that you can help bring about a better world.

For a good society is produced only by good individuals. just as truly as majority in a presidential election is produced by the votes of a single electors.

Everybody can do something towards creating in his own environment kindly feelings rather than anger, reasonableness rather than hysteria, happiness rather than misery –

Bertrand Russell.

There are few countries in the world I admire. These countries have indeed proven to the world that change and transformation is possible. They have shown the world that it is absolutely possible to transform from nothingness to greatness. Some men in this country took the initiative to take the bull by the horn, and they caught revelation of what could be.

They embraced it and poured it out to the entire nation. Today, these countries have become the pride of the world and of course envy of neighboring countries. I will limit my lists to countries that were regarded as third world some 20 years ago, who have diligently pursued their dream of becoming a better nation, and today, they have worked themselves into world great economy.

44

The table below represents the list of countries consistently considered Newly Industrialized Countries (NICs) by different authors and experts. Turkey and South Africa are classified as developed countries by the Central Intelligence Agency. Turkey was a founding member of the Organization for Economic Co-Operation and Development (OECD) in 1961 and Mexico joined in 1994. The G8+5 group is composed of the original G8 members in addition to China, India, Mexico, South Africa and Brazil.

Note: Green-colored cells indicate higher value or best performance in index, while yellow-colored cells indicate the opposite.

Source: Wikipedia

http://en.wikipedia.org/wiki/Newly_industrialized_country

Region	Country	GDP (PPP) (Billions of USD, 2011 World Bank)	GDP per capita (PPP) (international dollars, 2012 IMF)	Income inequality (GINI) 2008-09	Human Development Index (HDI, 2013)	GDP (real) growth rate as of 2013
Africa	South Africa	555,340	11,302	63.1	0.629 (medium)	2.5
North America	Mexico	1,659,016	15,300	48.3	0.775 (high)	3.9
South America	Brazil	2,309,138	12,038	54.7	0.730 (high)	0.9
Asia	China	11,316,224	9,146	45.3	0.699 (medium)	7.8
	India	4,469,763	3,851	32.5	0.554 (medium)	6.5
	Indonesia	1,223,488	4,956	36.8	0.629 (medium)	6.2
	Malaysia	447,595	16,942	46.2	0.769 (high)	5.6
	Philippines	424,355	4,264	43	0.654 (medium)	6.6
	Thailand	622,914	10,823	40	0.690 (medium)	6.4
Europe	Turkey	1,288,638	15,029	39	0.722 (high)	2.6

These countries some decades ago where classified or categorized as third world, but today are in the categories of *New Industrialized Countries*. This transformation or national development started as a nebulous idea in the mind of one man, who through clear understanding was able to share and build a formidable team of leaders who together passed on this ideal system and dream and it suddenly became the mission of the entire citizens. I took some time studying countries established or founded upon noble ideas and dreams, the United State of America holds the frontline for the rest of the world to emulate in this regard, see below the dreams and idea of some countries and how it has molded the civilization we all admire in these countries today.

The American Dream

Founding fathers of the American dream: George Washington, Thomas Jefferson, Abraham Lincoln, Theodore Roosevelt and Benjamin Franklin.

The American Dream is a national ethos of the United States, a set of ideals in which freedom includes the opportunity for prosperity and success, and an upward social mobility achieved through hard work.

In the definition of the American Dream by James Truslow Adams in 1931, "life should be better and richer and fuller for everyone, with opportunity for each according to ability or achievement" regardless of social class or circumstances of birth. The idea of the American Dream is rooted in the United States Declaration of Independence, which proclaims that "all men are created equal" and that they are "endowed by their Creator with certain

47

inalienable Rights" including "Life, Liberty and the pursuit of Happiness. The American Dream is the pursuit of happiness. We are not guaranteed happiness, but we are guaranteed the right to pursue happiness, in whatever way we might be able to (physically, spiritually and emotionally)

We are not content to have a disadvantaged segment of society and are always working on programs to bring them into the fold. Having rejected the concepts of royalty and caste, one is able to move freely to fulfill any goals, success, or lifestyle they are willing to work for. *(The America Dream)*

In Summary the America dream is:
- *To be free*
- *To be in Love and be loved*
- *To be healthy*
- *To not want for anything*
- *To be able to help others when needed*
- *To feel good about themselves*

48

- *To find someone that can rule this government for its good and the peoples and NOT themselves*
- *To find a new kind of fuel*
- *To solve the world's problems of hunger and education*
- *To be HAPPY, HEALTHY, LOVED and needed*

America's Founding Fathers clearly understood that faith in the Creator and true Freedom are inseparable. We believe their worldview was a Christian one based upon the Great Commission of the Gospel and biblically enlightened self-government. As inscribed on the Liberty Bell, *they would "Proclaim liberty throughout all the land unto all the inhabitants thereof." (Leviticus 25:10)* Solomon once said: "When there is no vision, the people perish."

The true American Dream is more accurately called "The American Vision". It is the Vision that drove our Founding Fathers to establish our Constitutional Republic as a nation under God. At the signing of the Declaration of

Independence in 1776, Samuel Adams, Father of the American Revolution, declared: *"We have this day restored the Sovereign to Whom all men ought to be obedient. He reigns in Heaven and from the rising to the setting of the sun let His kingdom come".*

In the final years of his life, Thomas Jefferson, author of the **Declaration of Independence** and third president of the United States, called upon the American people to

"Preserve inviolate the Constitution, which if cherished in all its chastity and purity, will prove in the end a blessing to all the nations of the earth."

As Americans we must also educate ourselves and our children in order to better understand our nation's founding documents and how America's Founding Fathers originally intended for them to be interpreted. Thomas Jefferson also said: *"If a nation expects to be ignorant and free, in a state of civilization, it expects what never was and never will be."*

Source: http://www.todaysamericandream.com

The Dubai Dream

In my research for countries consciously working themselves towards first class nations, I stumbled on an article about the Dubai dream online;

Today we approved Dubai Vision 2020 for the tourism sector. The goal is 20 million tourists & AED 300 billion in tourism revenues annually by 2020. We'll achieve this through 3 key areas of focus: family tourism, global events & attractions, & Dubai's status as a business destination. The vision is clear, infrastructure is ready & confidence in our human resources is high. The future does not wait for those who hesitate. We want everyone to work as one team to achieve the goal, with positive energy, strong determination & the belief that anything is possible.

Dubai model" the vision of one man **His Highness Sheikh Mohammed bin Rashid Al Maktoum** *Key achievements and directives of HH Sheikh Mohammed.*

Sheikh Mohammed embodies energetic and successful leadership. He is a man who has made promises and kept them; he has insisted on excellence and achieved nothing less; he has defined the role of leadership and fulfilled it. Thanks to his vision, Sheikh Mohammed has competently authored the Dubai success story and put the UAE on a unique path, which nations around the world compete to replicate.

Sheikh Mohammed has come up with several directives and laws aimed at providing a decent living to the nationals and residents in this country. He turned his attention to people, inspecting projects and following up people's concerns across the UAE. He inspected progress in all emirates, met residents and ordered changes that needed to be carried out. He undertook groundbreaking initiatives at an astonishing pace. The past few years witnessed unique achievements for Sheikh Mohammed both locally and regionally.

In February 2007, he announced the Dubai Strategic Plan 2015, which aims to bolster Dubai's leading position in the region and boost its role as an international economic and financial hub. The strategy will be used as a road map for development in the coming years. On April 17, 2007, Sheikh Mohammed unveiled the UAE Government Strategy Plan with the aim of achieving sustainable development throughout the country, investing federal resources more efficiently and ensuring due diligence, accountability and transparency across federal bodies.

Regionally, his most outstanding achievement was the launch of the Mohammed Bin Rashid Al Maktoum Foundation, on May 19, 2007, with an endowment of $10 billion. The foundation's aim is to promote human development by investing in education and the development of knowledge in the region by cultivating future leaders in both the private and public sectors, promoting scientific research, spreading knowledge, encouraging business leadership, empowering youth, renewing the concept of culture, preserving heritage and promoting platforms of understanding among various cultures.

Sheikh Mohammed launched Dubai Cares on September 20, 2007. The campaign, which raised an unprecedented Dh3.4 billion in its first two months, has become one of the biggest international humanitarian movements to focus on fighting poverty, spreading knowledge and providing education for children in the world's poorest countries. On September 3, 2008, Sheikh Mohammed unveiled the Noor Dubai initiative aiming to deliver preventative eye care to over one million people in developing countries.

This move is part of a drive towards a world free from curable forms of blindness, with the number of traffic deaths in Dubai rising, Sheikh Mohammed called for tough measures against reckless drivers. Sheikh Mohammad also stressed the vital need to develop education. He issued a law setting up the Dubai Foundation for Women's Development, which was tasked with developing and utilizing the potential and capabilities of UAE women. In an effort to encourage innovation, Sheikh Mohammed has announced a wide array of awards both in Dubai and the UAE, including the Arab Journalism Awards, the Dubai Government Excellence Program, the Dubai Holy Quran Awards and the Young Business Leaders Awards. These awards have promoted a competitive climate for both the public and private sectors to strive for excellence. Sheikh Mohammed also issued a directive mandating builders and developers in Dubai to comply with green building standards to ensure a healthy and environment-friendly city.

The past few years have witnessed significant progress in economic and social development: e-government was introduced; Dubai Metro was inaugurated and a significant number of investment companies were established. These companies have formed global partnerships in the fields of industry, commerce, tourism and sports and real estate management. Sheikh Mohammed set out his comprehensive worldview in his book 'My Vision', where he describes his philosophy and his political and economic vision. He also offers a detailed account of how Dubai and the UAE have been guided to their present-day status as international Centre's, renowned for their high quality commercial and financial services, luxury tourism and their drive towards sustainable human and structural development.

Through generosity and dedication, Sheikh Mohammed has achieved notable success while shouldering the great responsibility of leading Dubai and the Federal Government. This is who you can call a dreamer.

The Chinese Dream

Another country forcefully advancing is China, virtually everything electronic, household etc. is produced from China, this nation has suddenly taken over the economy of the world, below is the China dream concept.

The Head of State of China, Xi Jingping explained his China Dream in his first address to the nation as head of state on March 17:

"We must make persistent efforts, press ahead with indomitable will, continue to push forward the great cause of socialism with Chinese characteristics, and strive to achieve the Chinese Dream of great rejuvenation of the Chinese nation. To realize the Chinese road, we must spread the Chinese spirit, which combines the spirit of the nation with patriotism as the core, and the spirit of the time with reform and innovation as the core."

The China Dream: Great Power Thinking and Strategic Posture in the Post-America Era. He believes Xi shares his dream to make China the world's dominant power. Compare the China Dream to the American Dream this way: The American Dream refers to the dream of the protection of individual rights ... The Chinese Dream is the dream of strengthening the country's rights. The China Dream based firmly on bettering Chinese society as a whole: correcting inequality, ensuring free education for all, improving the quality of food, air and water, the China Dream is truly both individual and collective.

The South African Dream

If there is any nation in Africa that Africans and the rest of the world would want to associate with, it's South Africa. My first time visiting this country, I practically was shedding tears, because it was absolutely unbelievable for me that an African country was this beautiful. For a moment, I thought I was in Europe, but it was and is still Africa. Sure, Nelson Mandela did not build South Africa, Europeans built South Africa for themselves, but through the foresight of a true leader, the structures and systems are evolving to favor the future of South Africa.

Nelson Mandela

Finally, the South African dream would never have been possible without, probably, one of the greatest men of all time, **Nelson Mandela,** some say he is a freedom fighter. Whatever your view, you cannot take away the fact that this man, through his hardship, courage, determination and leadership, inspired a multi-cultural nation for the better. There is so much said and written about this incredible man, I think the quotes below says it all from a wider and personal perspective.

A Poem That Inspired a Nation - Invictus

*Nelson Mandela was imprisoned on Robben Island in 1964, and was the 466th prisoner to arrive that year. The prison administration's scheme of numbering prisoners was to follow the sequence number of the prisoner (466 in his case), with the last two digits of the year (64). The prison imposed the number on him for over 25 years, until his release in 1990. **"Prisoner 46664"** continues to be used, as a reverential title for him, and the Nelson Mandela Foundation uses 46664.com as its website address. While incarcerated on Robben Island prison, Nelson Mandela recited this poem to other prisoners and was empowered* *by its message of self-mastery. It was also used in the powerful biographical film, of that name, released in 2009. English poet William Ernest Henley wrote this short Victorian poem in 1875.*

Out of the night that covers me,
Black as the pit from pole to pole,
I thank whatever gods may be
For my unconquerable soul.

In the fell clutch of circumstance
I have not winced nor cried aloud.
Under the bludgeoning of chance
My head is bloody, but unbowed.
Beyond this place of wrath and tears
Looms but the Horror of the shade,
And yet the menace of the years
Finds and shall find me unafraid.

It matters not how strait the gait,
How charged with punishments the scroll,

I am the master of my fate:

I am the captain of my soul.

http://www.capedreams.net/info.asp?db=information&category_id=34

For the rest of the nations in Africa, who will dream for us? Unfortunately, the crop of politicians we have today have not in any way done us any good, because with every bit of action, they have proven they have a much more personal agenda rather than a collective people oriented program. You are the change Africa is been waiting for. You are the change your country is waiting for, and you are the change your family needs, how do I know this?

If you have read this book thus far, and you are still thinking of one gladiator and superman who will come save your country, then I guess you better start looking inward, because that superman, that gladiator might just be you.

If at any point of your life, you have thought about or perhaps considered or conceived a solution capable of resolving the issues of your country better than what the government is doing, that means, there is a voice in you that believe change is possible; the gladiator in you is calling for your response to go save your country. In my personal opinion, I will say it's time you began preparation; because one day, you might just wake up as the president or the leader of your community. I learned it is far better to prepare for an opportunity or responsibility and not see it come, than for it to come and not to be prepared.

There is a generation that understands what it means to dream; I believe you belong to that class of born leaders. A breed of renewed and transformed leaders destined to carry our nation and continent to the next phase. You have what it takes to dream and pass down a life filled with purpose to the generation following, something inside of you is already beckoning the burden to fight and stand for what is right and fair. The belief that Africa, your country, your family and your life can take a turn to greatness is dependent on you.

I wrote this letter specifically to you, because I know that the day you will find it and read it, That's the day change begins, for vision and dreams reveals inside of you the picture of what can be, and the desire and willingness to pursue will birth noble ideas, character, integrity, selflessness, purpose, innovative leadership and hope for a better tomorrow.

In your pursuit, I owe you a great deal of insight to understand that the common man's dream may differ from the uncertainties of politic and policies, but visionary leadership will help the common man feel great and happy when his own dreams are fulfilled.

Many shortsighted leaders have confined the needs of the common person to become their own dream. That is not what visionary leadership will do; you do not provide just food for the common and poor in the society without making plan for how to teach them to make their own food.

Visionary leadership will help the common and poor man consider the greater gain of putting his needs secondary to the fulfillment of a greater and global ideology, which will benefit not just him, but his generations unborn. In as much as we pursue the bigger picture, dreamers empower and create system that can make possible the following for the common in the society.

- *Education without tuition*

- *Employment*

- *Doctors that don't sell medicine*

- *Food without poison*

- *News without lies.*

- *Government officials without bribery.*

- *Police that do not abuse citizens*

- *Homes that don't get demolished*

- *The people don't fear authority.*

- *Environment without pollution*

- *Leadership without special treatment.*

Of a truth, a system and government where all things work

perfectly does not exist, but a leader who can help achieve some of these listed needs of the common man in the society is the man that the people will forever honor. That man must be a dreamer to achieve these great measures of success for a nation. Are You That Man?

One man with a keen understanding of vision that made a difference is Singapore's minister *Lee Kuan Yew.* Yew turned a developing nation into one of the world's most developed countries. Singapore is often referred to as the Switzerland of South East Asia, thanks to his leadership and unswerving determination.

According to *National Geographic Magazine,* in an article titled "The Singapore Solution" It is stated that Singapore's per capita income for its 3.7 million citizens exceeds that of many European countries, the education and health system can compete with anything in the West, government officials are pretty much corruption free, 90 percent of the households own their own homes, taxes are relatively low, the streets and sidewalks are pristine and you do not find homeless people or slums. Singapore also boasts of an unemployment rate of less than 3 percent. Singapore has often been referred to as "an economic miracle", because it has achieved so much, in such a short time.

On the 5th of June, 1959, Lee Kuan Yew, a prominent member of the People's Action Party became the first prime minister of a pre independent Singapore and remained in his post for twenty six years. In 1965 when Singapore finalized its independence from Malaysia, Lee Kuan Yew had his work cut for him. He started out with what most leaders would consider an impossible undertaking.

When Lee Kuan Yew was head of an independent Singapore, one of his first tasks was to have the sovereignty of Singapore recognized by the United Nations. In September 1965, Singapore joined the United Nations. He believed that government officials should be well paid, in order to curtail corruption. He also felt that an overgrown population would threaten economic progress. Therefore, he developed the Stop at *Two Family Planning Campaign*. The Stop at Two Family Planning Campaign was an aggressive method of discouraging rapid population growth, by urging families that already had two children to undergo sterilization. Let just say, it worked a little too well.

At the current time, Singaporeans are simply not reproducing. With a fertility rate of 1.29 and not a whole lot of intercourse going on, Singapore population growth is largely dependent on immigration. At the present time, in order to prevent the extinction of the Singaporeans, the government is even giving married women baby bonuses for having three or four children. Extremes are bad, especially if family planning policies are misguided. Economic growth is encouraged by what some Singaporeans refer to as the "big stick and the big carrot."

Everyone can see evidence of the big carrot, by simply witnessing Singapore's impressive economic growth. The big stick is another matter, this is done by creating and enforcing many rules that are foundational for a well-ordered nation. When entering the country, on each airport entry card, it is stated in read letter that the penalty for drug trafficking is "DEATH."

Minister Yew describes human nature as being animal like. He believes that man can be trained and needs to be disciplined. This is accomplished by lots of rules. The enforcement of these rules is quiet strict. They are enforced with anything from fines to occasional outings. They also believe in practicing corporal punishment. In Singapore caning is mandatory for at least 42 offenses.

Disruption in religions is simply not allowed. In order to preserve racial harmony and avoid many of the riots that had separated the country back in the 1960's, the government installed a strict quota system in public housing to make sure that ethnic groups do not create their own monolithic units. Whether or not, this is government sanctioned, this has been a very successful way of keeping different ethnic groups from being pinned against one another. Singaporeans are so excessively compliant with the many rules that they have the rules internalized. One resident calls it "the cop inside our heads." This has diminished the need for police surveillance. There is almost no theft, nobody steals wallets or engages in acts of vandalism. This is a country where conformity is commonplace and self-censorship is a very common practice.

Source: http://internetwriter62.hubpages.com/hub/Singapores-Transformation-from-a-small-Struggling-Island-Nation-to-a-Thriving-Metropolis

So, I wouldn't be out of place to say; If Singapore, China, Dubai and the rest uprising economy could find a way out of poverty Africa too can…

4

Change!

The lack of knowledge is the beginning of folly, says the wisest king that ever lived. Honestly, one of the greatest misery that has befallen mankind is the inability to say things the way they are. The next biggest idea the world is searching for is the ideal of truth, for with truth, comes freedom, liberty and unconditional love. All these are what humanity wants.

Nobody can do anything against the truth. Fighting the truth only calls for deeper attention on the truth, with time the truth always reveals itself, so is change. In as much as people, systems or culture wants to fight against change, time is changing and change is happening rapidly, the ineradicable consequence is that those who fight against change are left behind. Change begins with a desire, desire creates the dream, and the dream creates the reality if pursued with all tenacity. It is imperative that if we must experience any form of change in our personal, public or political system, we must desire it.

What Really is Change?

Change is the *act* or instance of *making* or *becoming* different. This definition is so complete and quite easy to understand, the word **act**, can simply be replaced with *"To Take Action"*. This means that change is *deliberate*, which means to be thoughtful, methodical, and meditative. Another outstanding attributes of change from our definition is that change is also the *'making'* this implies change can be created. I will redefine change as *the ability to take thoughtful action in order to create the life we want.*

71

- *Change can also be a redemptive measure, a force deliberately positioned in order to get someone out of something/state/place to where he ought to be.*
- *Change is a positive fight for your life to experience your desired objectives for living.*

It's always been a tough brawl when change is introduced into any system, be it our personal life or society. One reason why I believe majority fights against change is simply because they are sometimes not anticipated or expected because they never desired it, so it seems sudden and unexpected. Another school of thought believes people would rather settle for that one bird at hand, than take the opportunity to catch two in the bush.

For these numerous reasons, many are living life below expected desires. Many are passing through life not finding the true meaning of their existence. Many are fighting their own destiny all because they feel comfortable. This attitude to our personal life is what has given rise to the passiveness we see in social responsibilities and public participation in politics and government. What makes the change we are discussing more meaningful is the fact that it spans beyond an individual's personal ambition for greatness; we are talking about change that leaves a lasting impact on the society at large. However, we leave in an ever dynamic world, our life is ever evolving, as knowledge increases, change begins to fight its way into our personal life and this becomes the reflection we see in the larger society.

Now, the word "change" is such an ambiguous word, we must narrow down to drive home the right message. I am well aware people change from being good to becoming bad, and some from nice and friendly society to a hostile one. Some from bad become good and better, although there is a law of cause and effect operating in the bottom line why people or systems or society change. It is ideal we be clear that the change I dream about is a *"continental transformation" aimed at repositioning the people of Africa, from mental enslavement, self-injustice, to a renewed and ameliorated people, equipped and empowered with intellectual prowess that will birth a new generation of leaders, who will be front liners in innovative governance.*

It is absolutely possible to transform from a third world country to becoming the best and wealthiest economy in the world, far above the United States, the EU, and China etc. And I believe someone reading this book at this stage could possibly be laughing at my high horse belief. *I guess I must be dreaming? Oh yes!* Dream is what it is, and in the nearest future, this will become our reality in Africa, if we will do what is required of us.

I have so much faith in Africa that if given the right enlightenment, tools, structure and governance, we can achieve more than we can imagine. But the irony is that nobody will give anything to us. If indeed, we really want it, we must create it. It will also be pointless and absolutely irrelevant to the purpose of this book to begin recounting to us what we all perceive as the problem facing this continent. In the earlier chapter, we discussed extensively the root problem of African leadership, we were able to identify that the lack of vision and absence of a purpose driven leadership are the real root problem of Africa politics. Some school of thought may have thought otherwise, majority actually believe corruption is the real deal killing Africa politics, but unfortunately, corruption is just the byproduct of lack of vision in government.

All we have called problems are simply the symptoms of a root cause. *Corruption is a* symptom of a major disease in our various nations in Africa, and unfortunately, we have actually tried to manage this disease through some medications rather than utterly removing it. Again, I give a lot of credit to the measures various governments, society and even any individual may have put in place to combat these cancerous epidemics such as corruption, lack of direction, greed and its likes. I believe if only they have a better approach and understanding to eradicating corruption, they will do better. If only they had a clue of what the root problem is; then dealing with it from the root would have been their best option. Any curious mind such as mine, would rather ask why things are the way they are? For Change is absolutely possible, but only to the degree we desire.

To that degree we must sacrifice for, I know there are a couple of minds already receiving and thinking in higher dimension for Africa. I can attest to the fact that people are springing up from various countries in Africa, and are positioning themselves for the change that is about to happen, because some of us know and are fully aware that our time to rise to the full manifestation of our endowed abilities and potential as a continent is now.

To enter into this new dimension, the need to fully understand what and why we have to change is also highly important, and this message of change must be driven home to the very length and breadth of this continent, where everybody becomes a major player and a champion campaigner of this great revolution. Our role as beloved citizens of this continent is simply to be the first to begin the change or make the **shift in our mind.** *Yes!* That is where the game change begins. We must consciously, deliberately, relentlessly and consistently pursue to change our thinking and idea about governance and government, and most importantly, ourselves.

Africans, like much of the rest of the world, believes politics is dirty, and so every politician plays dirty. Truth be told, from the definition of politics, I don't see a place or word that connotes dirt or filthiness, because politics is simply *the academic study of government and the state,* also *the activities of governments concerning the political relations between countries.* Now this brings me back to the words of Shakespeare *'that nothing in itself is good nor bad'* but the vessels or individual involved are the factors that determine if a thing is bad or good. Political players brought deviousness to politics and hence, it's been termed a dirty game. The game in itself is not dirty, but only has been played by men and women filled with filth. But from this moment, you and I have got to decide to take back our place in the affairs that determines our economy, security, wellbeing and the future of our children.

The change spans from our mental transformation through taking responsibility of our government system. It's time for true leaders and people of integrity to embrace and venture into politics. It's time for the dreamers, visionary leaders, men and women who are blessed with administrative acumen to rise up and pour out the ability wrapped within and around them for the purpose of repositioning our nations in Africa.

At this juncture, we must be clear; my advocacy for change is certainly not a clamor for violence, and neither is it opposition with terror, for political violence has not in any way been the best approach to getting problems solved. Even if some result are forcefully attained it ends up destroying more than was ever planned or envisaged, violence is a destroyer, a massive dis-enfranchiser, and certainly not a reasonable approach to bringing about change.

Africans need a miracle of the mind; we must welcome a new culture of reasoning and a transformed thinking life style that generates vision and purposeful leadership. For a continent with the most endowed natural resources, full of wealth and abundance, and yet wallows in poverty, there must be something we are not doing right. We must be lacking foresight!

I learned from a very close friend, that the key to national development is in personal development, this is such a great statement. If this line goes directly by it's meaning, I must then begin with myself before pointing at people or system or government. The biggest issue with us in Africa is that we have failed to take the responsibility gawking at us. The average person in my country Nigeria is quick to lay blame on another person. We are so quick to blame the government for anything, even when our children fail their exams, the first point to blame is the government. I beg to differ. If not all, almost all African countries are the same as mine, there is no continent without the countries. Likewise, there are no countries without the people, so at every point in time, whatsoever it is that you do reflects the image or picture of your country and continent.

You are your country, and you represent your continent, the way and manner you comport yourself is exactly the way the world sees your country and your continent. This is where the shifting starts. This is where change begins, we must change the way we think to become the person we want. Our understanding of politics in Africa is based on selfishness, cartel ambition and not vision founded upon the need to serve. Are you ready for change? We cannot provide any meaningful solution to a problem, with the same mindset that created it.

Switching For The Shift

5

*W*hen viewed in an inertial reference frame, an object either remains at rest or continues to move at a constant velocity, unless acted upon by an external force. This is Newton's first law of motion and is one of the greatest lessons of life that I have learnt. Absolutely nothing changes unless a force is applied to cause a change. And a force is always deliberate; a force is a push or pull that can cause an object with mass to accelerate or its movement be altered.

I may have been talking too much of physics here, but these high school lessons are coming much more alive to me as I unravel the mysteries behind switching for the shift. As the people, we represent the mass, we have the unquantifiable weight required to transform our nations, and our acceleration or deceleration is solely dependent on our willingness to apply the force of change. That willingness is the point of switching because there is no government anywhere without the people, and so the people must be willing to play their roles.

These roles begins from a mental shifting, one of the responsibilities towards shifting is that we must appreciate knowledge about government, for *if a nation expects to be ignorant and free, in a state of civilization, it expects what never was and never will be.* At this very juncture, we must rise up not only in words expressing our disappointments to the roles people in government portray, but also in full readiness to unseat purposeless leadership in Africa as a whole.

You must be aware that we cannot in any way solve a problem with the same mindset that created it. This is where the real work begins, the point where all imagination, thoughts and strategic planning are put into positive and progressive action. The switch has actually begun for us on this continent. If you would be sincere to yourself, you may have noticed various groups springing up, a much more concerned generation for the well-being and management of the African resources are forcefully screaming change in their various and diverse capacity. Some foundations that are championing the cause of change and repositioning for this continents already exist.

I feel so proud being a part of some of these groups championing change for this continent, Africa 2.0, Nehemiah Project, SOFT Foundation, including numerous that I am not even aware exist, but are forcefully advancing and advocating one aim which is projecting the new Africa dream. These various groups have in a way reignited the passion for purpose and pursuit for a transformed thinking generation of Africa, whose core objective will be moving from the point of ideas to implementation. My philosophy about a people driven system of government is about models of a 'true people oriented' democracy. At this very stage, it has become vividly clear that the open neglect of the people's choices and voices has caused a lot more damage than envisaged. One vital solution that I strongly believe will eradicate government shutdown, violence, war and rebels is an institutionalization of a true democratic people oriented and people driven system.

If democracy is indeed what we were taught back in high school, then mirroring from a corporate paradigm, my concept of people-driven leadership, which I call People-Cracy, simply identifies and recognizes the people as the board of directors of every nation supposedly *practicing democracy.* Imagine your country as an organization, and you are a member of the decision making board! As a people meant to be owners, we have unfortunately become enslaved in our own land. Deeply oppressed by our own people, and occasionally when we are presented with the opportunity to change our destiny through electoral processes, we often find ourselves rationalizing and downplaying the importance of our future by the choices we make. There have been a lot of myth that depicts politics as a business of a certain class of individual, tribe, faith or race. And the greatest culprits to this irrational reasoning have been the Christians.

Some Christians have been taught and they have come to believe a true Christian should never meddle in the affairs of politics. Where and how these lies got its way into the Church is what I'm yet to unravel. This misleading concept must be completely eradicated, especially in the mind of Christians. Politics is for all; the shift must begin from our mind to reflect our true belief that change is possible.

All we need are people with the right frame of mind, prepared and trained to govern, and these class of people can be anybody who possesses the right quality, character and attitude to lead, someone knowledgeable and courageous to initiate change in our nation, because what you need to be a great leader has nothing to do with your background, culture, faith or class. Therefore, I believe I have spurred you enough to know, that you have what it takes to make a difference and further take this continent where it ought to be. That very first step begins with your perception and paradigm, your mind have to be reconfigured for the next level.

I hereby employ you to engage your imaginations positively, for it knows no bound, your mind has the capacity to conceive and create the reality of your life. The switching for the shift can only happen when you and I have decided to flip our minds positively, progressively and purposefully. The reality must first be created from the imaginary. This may sound like a writer's instinct exploring his fictional skills, but if only you know better, you will do better. The reality is that your countries and mine have suffered immensely for sheer lack of knowledge of who we are and the amount of power and influence we possess as the commonly referred masses. In some nations, we are actually referred to as the poor masses. If only we have an idea of the enormous advantage we have in terms of strength and number, we will be applying them rightly. We must consciously make a shift from that position and perception that has been used to define our life and future by insensitive leaderships.

It is imperative to understand that Ignorance of purpose does not in any way deny the existence or importance of purpose! You have not really lived except you have found the purpose for living.

Being born is because you carry in you some of the solutions that will heal the land. Switching for the shift begins with you. Somebody will have to take responsibility for building a better nation. We are no longer going to sit and lay blames. That's what losers do, and that's what we have been doing since inception. We have blamed the Europeans, we have blamed politicians, and we have even blamed the devil. Today, a shift begins with me, and if you are ready for this great dimension and new Africa, you must join this great cause, and take responsibility, because as true leaders, we take responsibility, we admit and learn from our faults, and most importantly, we take positive actions. Visionary leaders do not seek for whom or what to blame. *"The cause is simply to raise a new breed of transformed and enlightened visionary leaders from our generation to lead our nations in all its spheres of government in Africa to the promise land".*

One fundamental starting point is to *change our perception about everything happening.* One of my core responsibilities is penciling down a teleological approach towards national development, and my goal is to *enlighten, empower and build positive self-esteem in the life of the citizens of all African nations with knowledge. Also reconfiguring a mindset that better understand who we are and the role we all have to play in achieving a vision and purpose driven governance.* The change we seek is a direct function of our thoughts, decisions and actions. For my call to responsive and responsible governance is targeted towards a class of renewed and transformed minded individuals, who first, acknowledge that there is a need for a change, and are willing to be the first to switch for the shift in their paradigm and who also carry in them the prowess to influence the mass majority to follow suit.

The contents of this book or material is not in any way advocating violence, for those who toe embrace violence are doing more harm than the projected good, and records have also proven to us all that terrorism capitalizes on violence to strike its venom of destruction.

Our goal is to build, develop, maintain and sustain a trans-generational ideology of purpose, peace, prosperity, growth, and freedom from a vision driven leadership. And to achieve these, our thinking has to be exactly what we want. King Solomon in one of his documents of wisdom said, '*As a man thinks, so he is'* this statement has been proven to be very correct and true, we are a product of our thoughts, and the way people read our thoughts are by either our actions or by our words. This also brings me to a logical conclusion that we are who we are today because of the way we have thought and have been taught to think in time past. If poverty, lawlessness, disorderliness, corruption, greed, strive, envy, insecurity etc. is prevalent in our society today, it's simply because those are the predominant components of our thought pattern.

To take a new form, to turn from the way we are to the way we want to be is not going to happen by just confessing it. I know millions of Nigerians who on a daily basis confess that Nigeria will be better, but that is only going to happen when Nigerians begin to do things right and in order, and the first step to that better day will only begin when we embrace visionary leadership and consciously repel the greedy system of pursuing how we enrich ourselves from the treasury of government. No matter how much confession is made, if the principles that follow or accompany transformation are not in place, nothing will change. For praying and positive confession alone can never produce the result we seek, as we pray and confess, we MUST back it up with actions strategically tailored towards the reality of our dream.

For transformation or change to occur, there is first a state of remorse, and a personal conviction to change from the individual. Believers of the Christian faith calls this process 'Repentance' a position or state where an individual is personally convicted and then decides to turn around from his old ways of living to turn to a new way.

There is a need to exchange the components of our thought pattern to reflect the kind of country and continent we dream to have and pass on to our children, this is why we need to begin with a switch in order to achieve the desired goals of this cause.

Why Should I Care?

Somebody must be questioning my concerns and guts to call for national responsibility. You sure do have the right to boycott, for I believe there are several reasons not to care about the happenings of your countries or the continent. Especially if things are going pretty well for you as planned.

You can actually afford anything you want. If the government can't provide electricity, you can afford to power your generator without thinking about how much it cost, and absolutely not be bothered about the environmental damage your generator causes. Or you probably are a beneficiary of the decay in the system of government, so trying to change what works for you might be a tall order that you are not willing to obey.

Alternatively, you can with ease relocate in search for greener pastures anytime, any day with your family, you may think you do not have reasons to care, you may believe you have worked and secured your future and that of your family members, so why bother? If this is your thinking, then I suggest you think again. Because, we are in one-way responsible each other, if things are good for you and not for your neighbor or brothers, things are not yet completely good for you. Great leaders think first about the wellbeing of others before theirs, so it's the leader in you that we are waking up to answer the call of responsibility.

I strongly recommend that you be the first to switch, why? Because, gradually, a class of the society called the poor are drifting to a place of panic that tomorrow will never be better unless they do the unthinkable. A time is coming and that time is fast approaching when the poor will rise against the rich battling for survival. A day is coming if things are not restructured, that the rich and their high fences will be brought down by the poor, these horrible days can be averted, if only you decide to care and make a difference today.

Walking on the street of Sandton, just close to Mandela Square, I saw a write up by my greatest motivator, Nelson Mandela, and I quote:

"Do not fight crime with guns; rather fight it with jobs."

This is absolutely true! I do think you have every reason to care. Please note, I have not concerned myself about politicians in this chapter, because at this very point in time, they are not really my motivation. I care about the masses, the poor, and one of the ways I believe I can impact this category is by enlightenment. Exposing them to the truth of the power their voices and opinions command.

These categories are very special. Some of the people in this category end up becoming the leaders who will seat at the helm of affairs of our nations in the future, what do you think they will produce if they are not tutored correctly about leadership and legacies?

Dr. Myles Munroe, said, we are a product of our environment, the books we have read, the people we have associated with etc.

These conditions are what shape the life we live and makes up the person we become. At this point, I personally can't blame any person in a political office for not knowing what to do or how to meet the expectations of its citizens. My reasons are simply because, as a nation, we have not put in place measures to raise or train the kind of leaders we desire. So it will be out of place to expect a child to behave like an adult when he is but a child.

In order not to sound like am building a justifiable case for the present day politician, I believe that as long as people who vie for political office lack an understanding of our expectations from them, they never will produce the kind of result we desire. So, blaming politicians in Africa is like spanking a child for picking up stuffs from the ground to eat. The child ends up crying but that does not stop the child from doing the same thing the next time, until the child grows up, he or she does not have an understanding of why the crumbs of biscuits or cookies can't be taken from the dirty floor. We seek leaders in Africa, and we have not established any leadership academies preparing people for political offices. We seek change, and we have not prepared the environment for change, as we desired. Our lack of preparation returns to us the present result we see.

For Insanity is found when a person does the same thing and expects a different result.

Today, I advocate for an adoption of certain tested and proven principles producing results in the corporate world into our democracy in Africa. However, this time it will be the masses that are taking the shift, making the changes, turning the tides, becoming more politically active, and the very first step is to 'Accept You Are Responsible' for what happens to your country going forward.

And someone is *probably asking what qualifies him or her as a decision maker of his country?* Consider not your background, class, race, or even pedigree. For I know, the key to national development lies in personal development. If the nation must change for the better, you and I must also change. Imagine how viral this can go if every one person who reads and accepts responsibility begins by changing. That change will go viral and in no distance time, you will see the changes, remember a country is made up of people, and "the people" is you and I. we must be willing to switch for the coming shift to occur.

If you are a citizen (by birth or naturalization) of any country in Africa, living in or outside, you are *'welcome on board'*. All you need to move is first an understanding and awareness of your true potential as a decision making member of state of your country. From today, ***you call the shots***, you ***dictate the tone***, we (the board) are the reason why they (public officers) have a job in the first place, so we have the power now to hire or fire anybody or group of people who will not run the affairs of our beloved business (nation) with our own vision and meet our core goal, which is to build for us a visionary and innovative system, profitable policies and sustainable development.

98

Today, you have come to the full knowledge and deeper understanding that your country is yours and that all the resources are right in your hand and you must account for every penny running in and out. You must also account for every citizens of this country because they are your primary responsibility. Now, what exactly will you do for a change as a member of the board of directors/trustee?

You must also know that your lack of initiative or ideas leaves the country in a very precarious state, therefore, you must deeply think through your points as you attempt to share your values on some critical questions I believe every true leader should ask and provide answers for before venturing into any public role.

My research in this work has in one way exposed me to some building blocks of some great nations. It begins with Vision based on Value and Belief.

Below are the values from United State of America's system.

99

10 Core American Values

Individualism

- *Belief that each person is unique, special and a "basic unit of nature"*
- *Emphasis on individual initiative*
- *Stress need for independence*
- *Premium on individual expression*
- *Value privacy*

Equality

- *Open society that ideally treats everyone equally*
- *Little hierarchy*
- *Informal*
- *Directness in relations with others*

Materialism

- *A "right" to be well off and physically comfortable*
- *Judge people by their possessions*

Science and Technology

- *Values scientific approaches*
- *Primary source of good*
- *Major factor in change*

Progress and Change

- *Belief in changing self and country*
- *Manifest Destiny"*
- *Optimism -- nothing is impossible*

Work and Leisure

- *Strong work ethic*
- *Work is the basis of recognition.*
- *Idleness seen as a threat to society*
- *Leisure is a reward for hard work*

Competition

- *Aggressive and competitive nature encouraged*
- *Be First (#1) mentality*

Mobility

- *A people on the move*
- *Vertical (social / economic) as well as physical mobility*

Volunteerism

- *Belief in helping others (related to equality concept)*
- *Philanthropy admired*
- *A personal choice not a communal expectation*
- *Involves associations / denominations rather than kin-groups*

Action and Achievement Oriented

- *Emphasis on getting things done*
- *Priority on planning and setting goals*
- *Tendency to be brief and business like,*
- *Practical*
- *Measure results*
- *Focus on function and pragmatism*

Source: http://www.andrews.edu/~tidwell/bsad560/USValues.html

From the above listed core values from the USA, you and I can attest to the fact that every American child is raised by default with these consciousness and understanding of who they are and their responsibility to the world. It is absolutely possible to replicate or create ours, no matter the level of decay in the system, change is first seeing from the inner eyes of one man before been translated for all to see, that one man could be you.

I have outlined a series of questions for you to provide answers. If you find yourself today in the position of leadership, creatively think and innovatively redesign your dream country, this could be your template for the change we dream of.

For what purpose is this nation founded?

✓ _____

_____

_____

What is my dream or vision for this country?

✓ _____

_____

_____

What philosophy and belief would I build this country on?

✓ _____

_____

_____

What are the core values of the country I want to build?

✓ _____

_____

_____

What are my short-term and long-term goals for my country?

_____

_____

_____

What strategic plans would I initiate to achieve my dreams and goals?

_____

_____

_____

If by any chance, you have completely answered all the questions above, then I want to believe you have probably given answers to the set of questions you may have in time past asked or thrown at politicians. You also may have probably written down the solution that your nation needs. Now that you have the opportunity, this is how and where responsible leadership begins. You have just written down a clear-cut vision, goals and strategy to reposition your country. You must also be aware, it doesn't stop here, we must find ways to make known our expectations to politicians, and if that measure does not work out well, one thing I have learned from some great leaders, is that when you want things done well, you go do it yourself. I certainly wouldn't expect anything less from you. If it will require you vying for a political office to make a difference, Go Do It!

For knowing the solution is not the problem of Africa and its states, but acting upon the truth that we know. Implementation has always been the fundamental barriers to the dream continents, now the question for you and I is 'how do I move from knowing what to do to actually doing'? How do I step into execution of the knowledge of what must be done? This is where I think some freedom fighters, activist and rebels miss it, and the position or route to implement a true national transformation has to be clearly defined. Again, this brings me to the place of personal commitment and shift towards change, because if the core values you have written down do not coincide with your personal life style, then we will be having major issues going forward. It is absolutely impossible to enforce principles and policies you are not ready or willing to comply with as a leader.

This is where and how switching for the shift begins with you, remember, national development is a direct functionality of personal commitment and development, so you and I are going to begin our shifting by consciously conforming to the true nature of the kind of country we want. It starts from the mind; you must see it happening, you must think about it happening, you must position yourself for it to happen.

Somebody may be asking; how on earth can his or her answers be the solutions that will solve ancient and inherited problem burdened upon our generation and nation by irresponsible and purposeless leadership? I have reiterated countless times that the core objective of this book, My African Dream, is solely to *enlighten, empower and esteem the citizens of all African nations with knowledge, better understanding about who we are and the role we all have to play in achieving a vision and purpose driven governance.*

What is most important beyond what I want to do is how I want to do it, and my simplest strategies are:

Educating African lower class citizens, by bringing them to the place of self-realization and awareness of the power they possess.

And my aim for educating is because I want to eradicate the myth that power belongs to a sect or class of people. I want all to be aware that anybody who decides to embrace and comply with the right principles of purposeful leadership, irrespective of class, background, tribes or race can become the conveyor of the change we seek in our various nations. I want to empower and infuse into these mass majorities the right vision, the right character and attitude, the right thinking for responsible leadership. I want to become a channel where something great can be carved out of nothing. I want to ignite the fire of purpose. I want to rekindle the hunger for change. I want to steer up the greatness lying fallow deep inside the subconscious of the so called poor, helping them know that they are not indeed poor as the society may have labeled them, that they only are suffering from their passing over of opportunity repeatedly which has placed them in a stagnant positions for long.

Why Choose Education?

Education from our schools today is not compact enough to produce the kind of geniuses with the capacity to lead. I speak beyond classroom literacy and discipline or professional intelligence, for various careers we all have acquired as a result of going to school. My sense and level of understanding for education is what governs how the school walls have affected our sense of judgment and level of reasoning, how it affects our choices and decision-making processes, how what we have acquired from school transcends to the larger society. By these, I mean, our education has not yet impacted or enlightened our society to the point of assuming roles of responsibility, our schools syllabus is deprived of leadership, vision and purpose.

Recall that sayings of Gandhi: *If you want a change, you begin the change and others will see and emulate you.*

Eradicating naivety is a long process that requires just only one simple step, which I believe, is quality education. It is knowledge or awakening or awareness that illuminates the mind. It helps the soul and heart of man unlock the hidden darkness and allows a clear distinction between truths and lies, can you imagine how well informed Africa will be if 95% are well educated and enlightened to knowing what is needful, good and futuristic for the nation?

110

Beyond sentiments, nepotism, tribalism and party discrimination, true patriotism is when a society becomes responsible for the state of its existence. This is a core switching for a shift. We must all go back to the basis to acquire the true knowledge and understanding of what leadership and supporting a leader is all about. We call it followership here in Africa.

My greatest heart-break for the nations of Africa is the point where followers, despite the fact and awareness of the incapability of the leaders they follow, despite the cruelty and ravenous nature of these leaders are adamantly following, even to the point of sacrificing their lives for leaders who do not have a single plan for the future of their followers.

Time has come when we as followers will put our interest first before the desires and promises of every leader; ignorance has demobilized and paralyzed our sense of judgments, our vision as followers is a function of the knowledge you and I have. The effect of our state of living as followers is directly proportional to the level of knowledge we have. As followers, we sure do know what we really want, but we just do not know how to get there, and that is why education and pursuit for knowledge is key and most critical to the realization of the kind of nations we want.

Every citizen must apply himself to learning, which can be a self-development program, learning about government and government processes, learning about what is expected from the followers and what is expected of the leader, and then only can we break the limitations starring at us in form of poverty. This learning is meant to be streamlined in the area of interest, and our core area of interest in Africa today is governance, we need to understand what true governance is about, because we must understand that our learning today, determines our earning tomorrow. If we can align ourselves to this fundamental essence of governance and understanding of the role we play as followers, then I can assure you that gradually, we will fizzle mediocrity that abound in our society. We will be enlightened to the point that we can discern from knowledge a lying politician, a purposeless and visionless leader, and a mere-talk politician who lacks strategic plan for implementing all the talks. In Africa politics of today talk is cheap and work is weak. Only an enlightened society can attain this level of intelligence and break free from looters and resource devourers, and this is the shift I proclaim for this continent. We must make the switch for the shift to begin.

I must at this juncture prepare you for the battle ahead; for the fact that you attempt to make a difference does not guarantee you will succeed or hit the target at the first try. The fact that you have great ideas, and vision for a better government is not a guarantee that people will support you. The fact that you are even trying to fight for the poor does not mean the poor will be in support of your ideology. So, it is better you come into this fight or battle better prepared and aware that nobody is going to give you the chance to even showcase the greatness locked up inside of you, nobody really cares about what you know or have to prove.

This is where great men are separated from ordinary men, greatness comes with a price, a price worth sacrificing even your entire life. Nelson Mandela and his crew sacrificed 27 years of their lives fighting for one great cause, "Freedom and Equality". So many died fighting for the cause they believed in, your ideology may not happen even in your lifetime. However, the sands of time would have imprinted your name as a great initiator, fighter and advocate for change that generations to come will remember and celebrate you for.

I encourage myself daily with a whole chapter of Og-Mandino's scrolls, especially the Scroll Marked III. It's centered on persistence, the fact that I have an idea to educate and empower by building platforms that will bridge the gap of information in Africa does not mean I will have a smooth sail. The fact that I have a dream to make change happen does not mean it's going to come easy, but one thing is certain, in the clips of my imagination, it was a happy ending, so for that alone, I encourage myself daily to keep pursuing what I believe in. I believe it will not be out of place to share my motivations from Og-Mandino.

The Scroll Marked III

I will persist until I succeed

In the Orient, young bulls are tested for the fight arena in a certain manner. Each is brought to the ring and allowed to attack a picador who pricks them with a lance. The bravery of each bull is then rated with care according to the number of times he demonstrates his willingness to charge in spite of the sting of the blade. Henceforth will I recognize that each day I am tested by life in like manner? If I persist, if I continue to try, if I continue to charge forward, I will succeed.

115

I will persist until I succeed.

I was not delivered unto this world in defeat, nor does failure course in my veins. I am not a sheep waiting to be prodded by my shepherd. I am a lion and I refuse to talk, to walk, to sleep with the sheep. I will hear not those who weep and complain, for their disease is contagious. Let them join the sheep. The slaughterhouse of failure is not my destiny.

I will persist until I succeed.

The prizes of life are at the end of each journey, not near the beginning; and it is not given to me to know how many steps are necessary in order to reach my goal. Failure I may still encounter at the thousandth step, yet success hides behind the next bend in the road. Never will I know how close it lies unless I turn the corner. Always will I take another step, if that is of no avail I will take another, and yet another. In truth, one step at a time is not too difficult.

I will persist until I succeed.

Henceforth, I will consider each day's effort as but one blow of my blade against a mighty oak. The first blow may cause not a tremor in the wood, nor the second, nor the third. Each blow, of itself, may be trifling, and seem of no consequence. Yet from childish swipes the oak will eventually tumble. Therefore, it will be with my efforts of today. I will be liken to the raindrop which washes away the mountain; the ant who devours a tiger; the star that brightens the earth; the slave who builds a pyramid. I will build my castle one brick at a time for I know that small attempts, repeated, will complete any undertaking.

I will persist until I succeed.

*I will never consider defeat and I will remove from my vocabulary such words and phrases **as quit, cannot, unable, impossible, out of the question, improbable, failure, unworkable, hopeless, and retre**at; for they are the words of fools. I will avoid despair but if this disease of the mind should infect me then I will work on in despair. I will toil and I will endure. I will ignore the obstacles at my feet and keep mine eyes on the goals above my head, for I know that where dry desert ends, green grass grows.*

I will persist until I succeed.

I will remember the ancient law of averages and I will bend it to my good. I will persist with knowledge that each failure to sell will increase my chance for success at the next attempt. Each nay I hear will bring me closer to the sound of yea. Each frown I meet only prepares me for the smile to come. Each misfortune I encounter will carry in it the seed of tomorrow's good luck. I must have the night to appreciate the day. I must fail often to succeed only once.

I will persist until I succeed.

I will try, and try, and try again. Each obstacle I will consider as a mere detour to my goal and a challenge to my profession. I will persist and develop my skills as the mariner develops his, by learning to ride out the wrath of each storm.

I will persist until I succeed.

Henceforth, I will learn and apply another secret of those who excel in my work. When each day is ended, not regarding whether it has been a success or a failure, I will attempt to achieve one more sale. When my thoughts beckon my tired body homeward I will resist the temptation to depart. I will try again. I will make one more attempt to close with victory, and if that fails, I will make another. Never will I allow any day to end with a failure. Thus, will I plant the seed of tomorrow's success and gain an insurmountable advantage over those who cease their labor at a prescribed time. When others cease their struggle, then mine will begin, and my harvest will be full.

I will persist until I succeed.

Nor will I allow yesterday's success to lull me into today's complacency, for this is the great foundation of failure. I will forget the happenings of the day that is gone, whether they were good or bad, and greet the new sun with confidence that this will be the best day of my life. So long as there is breath in me, that long will I persist. For now, I know one of the greatest principles of success; if I persist long enough I will win.

I will persist. I will win.

For the cause is a tough call, but greater is the result to be achieved than the pain I will go through to see it come through for me and the next generation, this is my commitment to myself, my family, my nation and this continent; Africa.

119

6

Comparing Governance

Building businesses in an ostensibly unpredictable political terrain has been an amazing experience in Africa, despite the insufficiency and lack of infrastructures in some countries corporate entities are thriving and massively increasing. Maybe we can attribute their successes to the diligence hinged upon a vision, strategically mapped out to ride on the available opportunities rather than the disadvantages.

Nonetheless, I can attest to the fact that there is a percentage progress in corporate governance success achievement when compared to democratic governance. I'd like to draw an analytical comparison, because of the vast difference in terms of the level of success between corporate and democratic governance. Haven't you noticed that in nations where there is an immense decay in governance, private or corporate organization are still thriving, meaning there are yet people running an organization to the point of achieving success? Some schools of thought may differ from my comparison, as politics and business are completely two different things in the context of our discussion

My reasons are very clear and simple. I believe it's time we made politics our business and not making business out of politics as the case is. Therefore it is imperative we find the Principles and Strategies corporate organizations adopt to attain tremendous and sustainable success in nations where political leadership and governance are woefully collapsing? It is also important we understand from the perspective of literal definitions what each of these systems of government we are comparing means.

Corporate Governance

It is the set of processes, customs, policies, laws, and institution affecting the way a corporation (company or organization) is controlled, managed or governed.

Democracy

Another term for democracy;

Equality, Fairness, Classlessness, Consensus and Republic

I still can recall my high school definition of the term democracy, defined as' *a government of the people, by the people and for the people.*

Another definition for democracy says it is a form of government in which the people govern themselves or elect representatives to govern them.

The word *democracy* is a combination of two Greek words, *demos* which means *people*, and *kratos*, which means *strength*. Therefore, from this root understanding, it is clear democracy is *simply the strength of the people, and not the strength of some people, as the case is today.* This simple definition places accent on the *"people"* This only means *leadership and governance are people oriented.*

But realistically, from what we have seen and experienced, governance has never been people centered in our present day government, the original intent for the adoption of a democratic rule was founded upon a measure to empower and strengthen the people, why? Because the nation is the property of its citizens, therefore, the power of any nation is supposed to be owned by the citizens. I want us to begin our comparison of these two concepts of governance from analysis drawn from their various definitions; secondly we will compare the results or end products.

Recall we have defined governance as the act, process, culture, system or the approach adopted to run a system. Therefore, governance deals with the algorithm or process of managing the people and resources, while democracy is the strength of the people. Over time we have seen democracy benefit only a sector and not the people in general, so the right question will then be, *why are the poor masses the victims of democracy?* This burden led me to observing the leadership and concept of governance in the corporate world, where things obviously work almost perfectly well, these success stories could be attributed to the mindset of the driving forces behind the business or organizations, now my angle of reasoning is.

If things can work in the corporate environment, is it possible to adopt the principles and concept of corporate governance into democratic government? Can the same efficiency and effectiveness be attained? Moreover, can similar result of success be equally recorded? My take is YES! It's Possible; therefore, approaching and running the affairs of a nation like it's a business can yield a more promising result, now we are in the realm of Politics of Business, this is where and how I came about the comparison theory between these two concepts of governance and leadership. Corporate governance is a type of leadership operated in corporate environment or business organization. This type of governance does not necessarily give decision making power to its employees or staffs, rather, absolute power and decision making is solely that of the owners or founders, whatsoever this group of people or owners decides affects the people serving or working in that organization.

It is a result oriented type of leadership because both the owners and the members of board of directors are all in it for *profits.* Anytime there is a shortfall on this objective, the board enforces change immediately, by first firing those who have not performed in accordance to the codes of the organization and then by hiring people who can deliver the mandate, *which is to get result! And that is made possible by'*

- *Making sure the right services and products are provided, which will win them customers and that is how the organization can win money.*

125

- *Making sure the products and services are well publicized*

Interestingly in corporate governance, the management does not completely decide for the board, they come up with ideas or strategies to produce desired results; the board would still have to approve. But reverse is the case when it comes to the concept of democracy where the people supposedly should own the power. However, that is not the case for democracy.

From my point of view, I believe Africa's kind of democratic governance could be likened to an abridged form of corporate governance, nothing would have been more rewarding if the nations in Africa are been run as corporate organizations with a vision and a mandate to succeed. The negative impact of this type of democracy practiced in our continent is that it is only benefiting a very few set, *this concept or practices from Africa has made me redefine democracy to be the government (power. control, resources) for a set of people,*

126

forced upon the general public or masses by a group called political godfathers and party funders, this is what I call African democracy.

"Imagine, if we can adopt completely the concept of vision and purpose driven leadership found in corporate governance and tailor it towards nation building and human capital development for our nations"

"Imagine appropriating the best practices from corporate governance into democratic rule"

From my own country's extrapolation, Politics is the biggest and fastest growing business in town, so the intent for politicians is not based on the desire to serve and provide solutions to mitigate the pending problem facing the people, rather it's to be served, create more problems and make more money.

Some things can be guaranteed if we will be willing to adopt best practices of corporate governance, such as structures, purposeful driving force etc. I believe if some common

127

practices when setting up or starting a new business were in place for a political office, where the visionary or the entrepreneurs are required to produce and provide potential investors with detailed and almost self-explanatory business plan, followed by a strategic plan explaining how the business and its missions will be accomplished over time. Maybe the present day politician will fully understand that the era of making business from a decayed political system is over.

For in a corporate organization, the would-be investor wants to know if you understand what you are talking about.

- They want to know how the entrepreneur plans on reaching his business goals and objectives.
- They want to know and evaluate the risk involved in the business.
- They want to understand your concept of market and business leadership, by going through the pedigrees the team put together to manage the

business.

- They also want to see your numbers, if it is indeed true, and how you plan on making those numbers a reality.

These are what the corporate world wouldn't joke about when it comes to investment. But, we seriously, do not look into all these factors when it comes to politics, if only we know, that as an investor put his money on any business, so do people, the public put their own time, efforts and resources to every election and government. But to move on to the kind of visionary and productive government I dream about, I believe we'll need to imbibe these practices into our political business system.

From an investor's point of view, we call it due-diligence. It's about time we create a workable structure and consciousness for political aspirants, such *democratic-due-diligence* will better help our system to develop properly and produce true leaders for the future.

Below are some of the qualities seen in corporate leadership that we can adopt in democracy.

Visionary Leadership

Vision is the key factor of any corporate system. In every successful business, the owners have something from within driving them so passionately.

Purposeful Pursuit

Purposeful Pursuit is an essential ingredient for success applied by any serious minded individual and corporate organization; the word purpose can mean so much. It represents the essence why you are pursuing your dream.

Goal Oriented

Goals in corporate vision are the day-to-day task of any vision driven leadership, for goals are step-by-step objectives or target set by leaders to help accomplish the bigger picture.

Strategic Planning

Strategic Planning is a requirement in achieving any objective, because it's never enough to know what to do, but having a well-laid plan of how to do it is what strategy helps organization achieve.

Hard Work

Hardworking People (staff) are the tools and ladder holders corporate organization utilizes to achieve the set goal, people who are ready to die for the cause of the organization.

Accountability

Accountability spans beyond monetary checks and balances. It is the first measure of a responsible government, because it calls for answerability, and there is no corporate organizations that jokes with this department of the business, at every close of the week and month in some cases, there are reports of both how the business and the workers performed.

Anyone serving or working under the organization is accountable to the organization. Each group or department undergoes certain audits monthly or annually, because every organization believes there is need for assessments and evaluations of how well and how close the management team is working towards the realization of the goals and objectives of the organization.

Accountability is a culture of responsible government and leadership.

If these qualities, attributes and concepts from corporate governance are copied and brought into our political business, then we have a high level of assurance that we can attain 85% success in leadership. Unlike democracy practiced in Africa, where objectives and goals are driven by greed and corruption. It is quite palpable that the mandate each selected leaders go to fulfill is the greed, desires and selfish ambitions of these members of board of trustees and not of the people.

In summary, corporate governance is a system that benefits a very few, who are regarded as the owners of the business or shareholders. These few elite determines the fate of the thousands of staff who have given their time in exchange for salary or monthly allowance for the materialization of the big corporate vision. For corporate governance, it's all about the vision and goals of the owners.

While a democratic system is completely people oriented, 'though democracy practiced in some nations of Africa has openly pointed us to the understanding of politicians. We still have the chance and choice to make a shift and create solutions if we compare and complement our decaying democratic system with a solution driven corporate governance approach.   One thing is clear in corporate organizations; the Vision is clear, Purpose is clear, and everybody working in that organization is clear. If we must inculcate these corporate attributes into our political business, we must be very clear of what it is we want.

7

Finding What Works

I have learned over time that nothing new exists. Everything that exists has existed before and that the world is just revolving in circles, thus this permits me to state that whatever a person plans to achieve, someone somewhere has in time past achieved similar, if not exact. Nomenclature might differ, processes might differ, and seasons might differ, but the truth remains they both might have been invented and structured to solving similar problems.

Initially this book was to be titled *Be A Copy Cat* and this resonated from the need to embracing the models the nations who has delisted themselves from third world into great economy and leading nations adopted to gain liberation politically and economically. If you are ready for these new horizons, then as board members there are patterns, characters, habits, lifestyles, and ideals expected of us. These are the qualities of trail blazing leading society, which I believe are fundamental paradigm required of us as the new board. For we have become a renewed and awakened people, who have decided and volunteered to give ourselves to learning and leading forward the people we want to serve in whatever capacity life gives to us.

Today, we are repositioned from the mind as a people who understand our roles in national development, and to be transformed into the nations and continents that are prospering, there are tasks and models we must all embrace, and these are:

- Finding The Essence Of Our Existence As A Nation
- Build A Vision Driven Government
- Redesign and Position Our Lifestyle To Better Represent Our Beliefs

- Finding What Works And Working On It.

If you may recall, I began the introduction of this book alerting you about what matters most, which for me, is about why and how to make a difference. So, for the highlighted point above, its time I share with you how I think we can find the essence of our existence, how we can build a vision driven government, how we can redesign, renew, and reposition our mind for it to reflect in our lifestyle, and how we can find what works for us as a people.

Finding the Essence of Our Existence as a Nation

Why are we a nation? How did we become a nation? Many may see this as a difficult task to tackle, and a majority would want to refer to the Europeans as those who may have the answers to this very question. Somehow, you are right, but believe me, the purpose for the Europeans merging dysfunctional and conflicting tribes together to make up a nation was best fitting for their own selfish interest, which I can tell, they have realized their profits long ago and probably may still be reaping the dividends, this time around from another dimension of colonialism.

I direct this question particularly to the founding fathers or freedom fighters of our nations. I see no country in Africa today under any physical colonial bondage. Perhaps, we may be suffering from policy colonialism, nonetheless, we presume to be a freed state. This means every country has in one way or the other fought and won independence.

If that is the case, then what exactly was the reason for the independence? Was it only for freedom, and self-managing our resources? What political scientists call self-government? Finding purpose is about knowing and understanding the reason why we are born, the purpose for which we exist, the reason why you and I were born as Africans, because, there is one choice my father always told us that we can never make for ourselves, and that is choosing who your biological parents will be.

So the fact that we were born to African parents, tells me there is a purpose, a reason that I must find, because finding it, means finding my destiny, finding destiny means I have found my life, and that places me in a better position to function in life.

If there is any lesson from this book you must keep to heart, it is the unveiling of the true position and power that you have under your prowess as true citizens of your country. You and I have become members of the board of national affairs for our country, for that was and still is our original position and right. But ignorantly, we were lost, displaced, and that made people who knew and understood hijacked the seat of government only for them and their children to rule, suppress, and eat alone the resources meant for everyone to share.

Nigerians call it national cake, the fact that it is a cake sure means it was never meant to go round. This awareness and enlightenment positions the citizens to be more important and more powerful than the politicians who in time past oppressed and robbed us of all our rights and possession from our motherland. I also would like to educate you about this position. It is the position where you are the boss, and the jury in charge, so, any day any person from these our responsible groups decides to vie for a political office, He or she relinquishes his power to become answerable to those of us, who are not in offices.

Politicians are likened to management consultants and staffs. So as much as we trust the judgment of a consultant, they still will have to carry us along and advice, it is our choice to choose from their pools of advice, and when a consultant or management staff is not delivering, we fire them. They are much welcomed back to their rightful place as members of the board after their tenure or duration of service is expired, so the board takes virtually all-major decision.

Build a Vision Driven Government

So our topmost priority now that we are on 'the board' is to find and understand the purpose why we are a nation, and if at all, tracing back to history got us nothing about purpose for becoming a nation, It is then pretty clear that destiny was only waiting for this day to come, we must collectively think to build or create the dream country we want. We must take this giant leap into the future, there is nothing stopping us to rebuild our nation with a purpose.

I can assure you, we are not doing anything out of the ordinary, and also we are definitely not the first to do so, Dubai, was created out of this kind of process called vision. After the world saw Dubai, nations are beginning to embrace the model that worked for Dubai and the UAE at large.

All *HH Mohammed Bin Rashid Al Maktoum of Dubai* did was to dream of a city that will add value to mankind, a city that would become the attraction of mankind on earth. The new

Dubai was founded on a vision to attract tourist from all around. That dream redefined the way things began to happen in the city. That dream redefined the style and type of infrastructure that would be allowed and approved in the city development. That dream city made Dubai open their doors to international communities. Today Dubai has become a must visit. Purpose, dream, vision, continuity gave birth to the new Dubai, this means same components for success that worked for Dubai can as well work for all nations in Africa.

Time is a great factor for purpose to become a reality. This is surely our time and season. The whole world can attest to the fact that the time for Africa is now. Signs from the divinity attest to this truth. Suddenly greatness is springing forth from this continent; Africans are today creating multi-billion dollar businesses that are in their own sphere bringing about transformation. Yet, we have not taken this change from the corporate spheres to our democratic and political system of governance. Politicians may have failed us countlessly before and sure got away with it, however, this time, we are a newborn with a difference, a new breed of change agents, and if the management (politicians) fails, our strategic repositioning for re–electing a new management to run and manage the affair of our organization (country) must be vision driven, value adding and world changing.

Redesign and Recompose Our Constitution to Better Represent Our Beliefs

Literarily, a constitution simply means the compositions of something. However, from our context, we are actually referring to a body of fundamental principles or established precedents according to which a state or organization is acknowledged to be governed.

What exactly do you know about the Constitution of your country? I can bet not 25% of the population knows exactly what the constitution says. My understanding about a constitution is that it ought to be derived and composed

143

from the core values and beliefs of a people coming together for a common purpose. There is a great need for many nations in Africa to revisit, re-evaluate and possibly recompose their constitution. This is now our collective responsibility as the new board members; we must rebuild and recompose our constitution to suit the future, to fit into the kind of dream country we want. It must be a constitution that has the capacity to accommodate the singular beliefs of a people, tribes and faith etc. and void of selfishness, class, race and tribalism as the case may be.

I recommend that the constitution be integrated into the school syllabus in every level of education. I also recommend that a leadership course be integrated at every level of our educational system. These are part of my rebuilding process contribution to help create that great nation we dream. You all must be aware that the average American knows the American dream. This defines how intelligent and actively enlightened the United States of

144

America's society is. Our citizens in Africa can also be as enlightened. If we are willing to embrace the models they have adopted in pursuit of happiness and change. Recall, we have looked into the type of government in corporate entities or private companies, and discovered the core for these types of organizations and what makes them succeed is nothing but vision, purpose, strategic planning, backed up by relentless implementation processes.

These models are evergreen and never failing. Vision that works for corporate entities also works for nations that embrace it. An individual who has not yet discovered his vision and purpose for existence is said to be an experiment, meaning the individual is living life without meaning. This is the case of so many nations in Africa.

So as a heritage of this great continent, I believe it's high time we birth the dream for change, dream for greatness, dream that someday, somewhere in the nearest future,

Africa will emerge as the greatest economy, and Africans will emerge as the producers of the greatest and most loving people on the surface of the earth. I believe that one day, Africa will become the safest place to live in. I believe that Africa will become home indeed. I believe that one day Africa will no longer be called a third world continent, but it will become a safe haven for the world and a land of plenty and abundance, where poverty and diseases no longer thrive, but a place where prosperity and love abounds.

I believe that one day, African education will be ranked amongst the worlds best. I believe that one day, Africa will be a continent with zero tolerance for corruption. I believe that one day, Africa will rank amidst the top two most developed continents in the world. I believe that one day, Africans, I mean the average children, will be born into wealth, because the nation has secured their rights and future from the abundance and revenue generated from the natural resources in the country. I believe that one day, it will become the pride of the western world to own an African passport. I believe that one day, Africa will rule the world economically, politically and spiritually.

Finding What Works and Working On It

Singapore, UAE and China did it. We also will, if only we embrace the models from the people who have gone through what we are going through now and came out of it better, bigger, wiser and smarter and sure came out successful. This chapter has inspired me to create my own **WWW**. Which is an acronym for *Working on What Works?* It is common sense to find what works and work on it.

I'm certain we are not the first to go through challenging times as a nation. Wisdom encourages us to seek for those who went through these processes and came out victorious, so that we can understand how they overcame. *For it will sure be an insane approach to be doing the same thing and expecting a different result.*

147

We must find what works. We must find what the people who have succeeded in this path did and work on them all, so many things have to change, approaches and expectations must change, and to begin, we must be clear about what we want as a people and as a continent. I believe the people wants to see the manifestation of promises, the people wants to see proven leadership earned from the marketplace. By proven, I mean men and women who have been trained and tested in their personal life, career or enterprise as successful leaders prepared to lead a nation as an organization, with an awareness of accountability. Political parties would be formed and be based upon ideology of nation building.

Our involvement this time around is not going to be business as usual. Why? Because the role we have taken up requires all hands on deck and it calls for articulate, creative, sacrificial, and responsive leadership. In a simple word I mean, a people bound by committed responsibility to make a difference for the today and tomorrow. So in pursuit of this committed commission, we must become a more politically active society, a society hungry for change, a society where education and educating the public as regarding governance and government activities will be like surfing the web.

We will be;

Enlightened, and been enlightened will birth in us, the hunger for change, which in its place births purpose, this purpose will recreate in us a more spirited people who are self-motivated, readily prepared, effective, result-oriented, and responsible and more involved in the affairs of government.

As owners of businesses, the need to become more concerned with the progress and outcomes of activities is essential, because our investment has to produce for us the desired dividends. In the corporate environment, the management consultants or staffs many times come up with a strategy to deliver the mandate of the board, but the board also come up with suggestions to the management for an approach which they know can provide for them the desired goal. This board has come up with a practicable solution that can produce the result the board requires faster and accurately.

We as board members of this continent has adopted an approach that we have seen and tested or proven to have work in other fairs of life, this strategy is being encouraged in corporate governance, in business world, even motivational speakers and life coaches encourage it, the scripture also advices we adopt it, and what is this strategy? It's called the *"Copy–cat"* strategy.

In the part of Africa where I'm from, men and women have become successful by simply copying a type of business. In as much as the fellow makes profit and he/she is successful, everybody jumps into that business. This breaks monopoly but ultimately everybody begins to enjoy some level of profit, because the population density is massive, so one entity may not be enough to serve all.

Let me share a scenario with you, the very first man who was inspired to package water in a sachet (popularly known as pure water in Nigeria) made his early fortune as the visionary, but today there are over 20,000 sachet water companies in my country doing pretty well, turning over at the minimum a sum of N2, 000,000 from sachet water annually. All they did was copy the vision. They didn't have to re-catch a fresh vision. They found what was working and they worked on it. In business and entrepreneurial environment, it is greatly encouraged to find what works and work on it. Therefore, this board will always be concerned for how the political parties (management consultant) or the candidate (management staff) wants to implement their plans.

Alternatively as a board we also have laid a plan B, which means we are very determined never to be stranded by clueless political gangsters, who may trick their way into political offices and when saddled with responsibilities to deliver on mandates, will have nothing whatsoever to offer.

Our Plan-B is to allow our political parties go borrow people oriented and nation building ideas and embrace the models of prospering nations who are already where we want to be. Borrow the road map; borrow their strategies and implement. One of the core essences of this chapter is to challenge you and me, who have concluded politics is a dirty game and only played by evil hearted men and women. Africa and the rest of the world may have painted politics to be so. The truth is that politics is neither a sport nor entertainment, as that is what African politics has evolved into. It has passed the era when it was a game, now it is in the era of entertainment to the very enlightened and less concerned citizens today.

We listen to the news and happenings around our politics and we laugh and mock the foolishness and insensitivities of our parasitic leaders. Unfortunately we are laughing at our own demise, these politicians are shipwrecking us, leading us to a point where we are been sentenced to death daily; while we laugh, curse and swear at the government our future is been decided daily in parliaments.

This nonchalant attitude is jeopardizing our nation. It has deprived our children the promised future. One major motivating factor for writing this book is to wake you up from the slumber. It's time to take our rightful place in the politics of our nation.

It's time for idealist, visionary leaders, men and women with noble and tested character to become the leaders of great nations in this great continent. The truth is that, the people who have either volunteered themselves to serve or those who devote themselves to serve our nation are those who lack game plan, except that they have their own game plan that will enrich and benefit them alone. My mentor Tonye Cole once said, if the real and enlightened people refuse to participate in the politics of their nation, 'cows and goats will rule, and the enlightened will have no other choice but to choose between the cow and the goat to lead them.

I have taken time to study American and the European politics, mediocre don't stand a chance, and the people who come out to pursue public professions are men who have built pedigree in other spheres of life, men tested and proven to be worthy and honest leaders, men and women who come before the nation with a master plan and blue print of how they want to make a difference in the politics as it benefits and affects the people, this also is another model worth emulating from prospering world.

I don't know about other countries, but in Nigeria, the majority of our politicians are those whose enterprises have only survived because they are been fed from the resources of government.

Men and women who have not successfully managed their personal and private life, people who have not successfully built one business without the aid of government, these are the people vying for political offices. People who think political office appointment are just a call to share out of the national cake.

It's time for Africa to enter into the position where people who desire to lead must qualify to do so, people with proven track records of true and effective leadership in their personal and private life. A wise child learns from the mistakes of others not to make that same mistake.

To achieve better result within shortest time limit, I have heard politicians say to us that we should stop comparing our democracy with that of The United States or The United Kingdom, because these countries are over 200 years old, so they have made same mistakes and they have learned from it and now they are better.

155

That to me is not true, because if we become as old as America and as ancient as the world is, as long as we don't apply the principles and models or policies which birthed the change and transformed state the whole world envies, there is no magic that can get the same result for us.

If you want to get the same result a successful nation or continents have, the simplest way is do what they did right. My candid advice, get so much involved, your life and future depends on it, save your nation, save this continent.

Africa and Classism

8

This chapter addresses the challenges inherited through classism in a developing society such as ours in Africa. Many of the troubles our nation has faced and still facing can be traced back and very much associated with economic imbalances which has in many nations given rise to economic revolution, when oppression and suffering becomes overbearing, times will always arise when the oppressed will fight back at all cost.

If we must move forward, classism must be nipped in the bud, so it is now our collective responsibilities to create a balance that will eradicate these inherent challenges. I also must let you know that classism is part of human nature, for

157

as much as a man can acquire to be or look or appear better than his neighbor, he would always want to do so, we must all understand that happiness and wealth is dependent on the ability at which a man is willing to work for.

The objective I hope to achieve is to annihilate the defect of a society purely dominated and governed by classism. When classism is not obvious, it's much easier for a society to move ahead and achieve better result in all forms of development. In any society where both the poor and the rich has rights and access to same shopping mall, same public places, same road, same quality of education, same healthcare, same rights of equality, then that society is ready to achieve its greatness as a collective force.

I have often heard this parable *that all fingers are not equal*. I believe the philosopher or aged man who coined that parable meant to say that every human being has a capacity to function, and that all men can't function at the same capacity and level. However, it becomes burdensome and frustrating when a finger labors so hard to its level and capacity and yet can't feel the touch of oil or taste of it. So my attention on classism and nepotism is born out of the irregularities and imbalances we see happening daily in the society, even the *bible said, if a man does not work, let him not eat, what now become precarious is when a man works and yet can't afford to eat.*

The cry for justice from this categories of people may be classified as envy or perhaps discontentment, permit me to disappoint and discredit your belief that defines the poverty of the poor in the society as a result of laziness and slothfulness, it will be a misconception to say all the poor in the society are poor because they are lazy or slothful. Majority of the rich people's sources of wealth in our society can be traced back to government and political plunder, these are the class of people who have not worked for the high-life they live, they have only benefited out of nepotism.

Politicians and public office holders have taunted the society by flaunting wealth that is illegally acquired from the national resource right before the eyes of the poor. Intelligent graduates struggle to survive because there are no jobs, we see children of Special Advisers and Ministers fly on private jets, partying and parading collections of expensive wines and women because they have free money looted from national treasury.

While entrepreneurs parade the streets with great ideas and business plan seeking 1/10th of funding to create businesses that will provide jobs, liberate the society from impoverishment and gainfully engage the youths of our society. Again, if the class and luxurious lifestyle is founded upon hard work and personal achievement due to the sacrifice paid for a better life through knowledge and skill acquired from quality education and creative ability, then anyone who envies these categories of people is no other than a thief. Nonetheless, we also must find a common ground to merge and relate, so that the effect and negative sides of classism will no longer thrive and further destroy our nations. To achieve these goals, all citizens must wake up to this collective responsibility. For the greatest tragedy of the African society today is that the mass majority fall within the low class, these are the very impoverished class which makes up about 75% of the populace, the rest 25% classes are between the average, rich and wealthy.

I have observed that close to 80-90% of the people involved in Nigerian politics of today where amongst the mass majority group some 20 years ago. These men and women were part of the people who cried 'woe to the government' they were part of the groups who suffered the same frustration, neglect and heat of impoverishments inflicted upon the citizens by corrupt and visionless leadership. However, what became interesting and at the same time surprising is that these few took a good and bold decision to be responsible citizens willing to serve the nation and give

161

their own best ability to make a difference, or perhaps it was just a pretense to find their way into the circle of government; I believe time has proven to all today what exactly their motives are.

Many would have thought that since these men and women knew how bad and tough life was for them some years ago, that serving the nation would have become a better opportunity and platform to right the wrongs of government in their own capacity and avenue to help others get out of the state of penury and lack. Rather, they have only used that platform to their own benefit, and only to enrich themselves and their immediate families.

These men and women who once wore the shoes of sorrows, who once felt the bitterness of men inflicted sufferings, who life and time has given them the chance to make a difference would have thought differently and behaved responsibly well to go fight for the cause of the mass majority. The simplest answer to this barbaric and brutal rage against

162

fellow men is because classism exists. *Classism is a differential treatment based on social class.* Many African cultures and policies have openly and conveniently promoted classism. Nigeria for instance, has made sure the poor do not have access to good and quality education; hence, they promote these barbaric acts through lack of payment of teacher's salaries. They consciously promote shutdown of educational institutions, the strikes have become part of politics, educational infrastructure drained to zero, and the budgets allocated for education is about 10.7% from its original 6% or 7%.

As long as a nation has a generation or class of people deliberately deprived of education, that nation has only created slaves amongst its own people. The people who run and control the affairs of government in Nigeria have, since the 1980's, done very well in achieving their game plan to keep the poor uneducated and unqualified by adamantly promoting classism through total neglect of the educational sector, and with this devilish crafted move, their children whom they have used the resources of the nations to send abroad to acquire the best education from the best institutions in the world come back to keep the family ruling empire going, while the mass majority, uneducated, unqualified are busy struggling to have a life, struggling to survive, barely cares about who governs him or her anymore, nor does he care about the policies.

In Nigeria, the Academic Staff Union of Universities (ASUU) shuts down every year since the last 10-12 years. What exactly could be the problem that no government has been able to resolve? I'm of the opinion that government does not want to resolve the educational problem in Nigeria and other parts of Africa, and why is that? Because the plan is to keep the mass majority perpetually benighted, unenlightened, uninformed and untrained; it has always been the secret of the wicked-wealthy in every society to hide information from the less privileged, because the difference that exist between the poor and the rich is the information and exposure the rich is privy to and the poor isn't. So access to quality education will in a way bridge that gap between the poor and the rich, because someday the poor who have been given quality education will already be positioned and prepared for a better life in the future, and once that opportunity comes, the poor grabs it, and life becomes a different story entirely. This happy ending for the poor man is what the wicked-rich man does not want to ever happen. So the rich's attempt to perpetually keep the poor man under, and in darkness is the laboratory where classism is formed.

Amazingly, when I researched about the literacy rate of each of the African nations, the results of my findings triggered another level of worry, because, they were totally in contrast with the present realities, and that on its own posed a deeper question to me; *Does Enlightenment go beyond Literacy level?*

Below is the result of my finding, a statistics of the ranking of African countries by their literacy rate. This entry

165

includes a *definition* of literacy and Census Bureau percentages for the *total population, males* and *females.* There are no universal definitions and standards of literacy. Unless otherwise specified, all rates are based on the most common definition – the ability to read and write at a specified age (10 and above). Detailing the standards that individual countries use to assess the ability to read and write is beyond the scope of this article.

	Country	Literacy Rate
1.	Zimbabwe	90.70
2.	Equatorial Guinea	87.00
3.	South Africa	86.40
4.	Kenya	85.10
5.	Namibia	85.00
6.	Sao Tome and Principe	84.90
7.	Lesotho	84.80
8.	Mauritius	84.40

9. Congo, Republic of the   83.80

10. Libya   82.60

11. Swaziland   81.60

12. Botswana   81.20

13. Zambia   80.60

14. Cape Verde   76.60

15. Tunisia   74.30

16. Egypt   71.40

17. Rwanda   70.40

18. Algeria   69.90

19. Tanzania   69.40

20. Madagascar   68.90

21. Nigeria   68.00

22. Cameroon   67.90

23. Djibouti   67.90

24. Angola   67.40

25. Congo, Democratic Republic   67.20

26. Uganda   66.80

27. Gabon	63.20
28. Malawi	62.70
29. Sudan	61.10
30. Togo	60.90
31. Burundi	59.30
32. Eritrea	58.60
33. Ghana	57.90
34. Liberia	57.50
35. Comoros	56.50
36. Morocco	52.30
37. Mauritania	51.20
38. Cote d'Ivoire	48.70
39. Central African Republic	48.60
40. Mozambique	47.80
41. Mali	46.40
42. Ethiopia	42.70
43. Guinea-Bissau	42.40
44. Gambia	40.10

45. Senegal	39.30
46. Somalia	37.80
47. Sierra Leone	35.10
48. Benin	34.70
49. Guinea	29.50
50. Niger	28.70
51. Chad	25.70
52. Burkina Faso	21.80

http://theafricaneconomist.com/ranking-of-african-countries-by-literacy-rate-zimbabwe-no-1/#.UotMEmQpZD0

Does Enlightenment go beyond Literacy level?

My take is a *YES!* Being enlightened and being literate are completely two different things, literacy level is about knowing how to read and write, whilst enlightenment is about knowledge, understanding, and skillful wisdom required to learn, understand and reason in dimensions beyond the ordinary; below is a clear difference in meaning of enlightenment and literacy.

- *Enlightenment is man's release from his self-incurred tutelage.*
- *Tutelage is man's inability to make use of his understanding without direction from another.*

How to read and write is the foundation for enlightenment. Interestingly, anyone looking at the table would perhaps have expected more to come out from Africa. The fact that people can read and write does not mean they have the knowledge to understand the politics of their nations.

The fact that they have been schooled to the higher education or university level does not also mean they have been nurtured well enough to understand the politics and system of government, how it affects them and what responsibility they have to play in making their nations better. If these figures are anything to debate on, for me, I see a potential force literarily ready to be ushered into a dimension of knowledge about governance and politics. The fact that in so many countries, a child from age 12 can comprehensively write an essay tells me that if that child is taught leadership, responsibility and integrity of politics, that child can make a difference earlier in life. It's obvious that the contents of our education was never designed or constructed to transform our states of thinking, neither has it been tailored towards responsible leadership, for if it was so, Zimbabwe ranking as the most literate society would not be one of the worst country economically in Africa and in the world.

My belief is that education spans beyond what happens within the walls of schools. But that education is what you do with what you have been taught. Again this will question what we've been taught. Our educational contents for schools need to be futuristic, leadership driven, and entrepreneurially conscious etc. It has to be relevant to our development as individuals and as a nation. I believe the

171

game plan is simply to keep the mass majority subjugated and incarcerated for the minor elite, social monsters and embezzlers to always dominate. This is classism, and if Africa continues with this discriminative culture, then we are sure heading for a collapse. Take a deeper look into your own country and tell me if there are no forms of oppression. It is everywhere in the world, it is also widely a culture in the western world. The difference is that the mass majority are still entitled to the necessities of life in the western and civilized or developed countries as compared to many countries in Africa, where the mass majorities are so deprived of the necessities and amenities of life, which are meant to be provided by government or structured system of government.

How can we put an end to classism?

Truth be told, classism will never be eradicated from any human subsistence, simply because there is an innate quest for dominance amid fellow men. This was never God's original plan for mankind, but somehow we have found ourselves in this man-made dispossession, inequality and intolerance. How can we put an end to classism? Or how can we ensure the mass majorities do not suffer from classism? How can we ensure the mass majority have access to the necessities of life and can afford a normal life?

In developed countries, systems have been put in place that avail the majority quality and standard education, comfortable and low cost shelter, access to loans to grow businesses and so many other things I can't start listing.

Apart from South Africa, I do not know if there are any other countries in Africa where the average citizen have access to good and quality education, healthcare and other social benefits provided by the systems of government? Though we hate the truth, today I consider the great *afro music legend a prophet*, who foretold realities of today some decades ago. Everything happening in Nigeria today has once been echoed and danced to by Nigerians, who are

173

suffering and smiling. Classism is an oppressive nature, and it's not a culture I crave to continue in Africa. My dream is to see an African state where everybody can relate, share and enjoy the basic necessities of life, where every citizen is entitled to same level of protection and provision by government, where our youths and children are getting the desired standard of education that can make an average African child stand on the same pedestal with an average American college or university graduate.

I look forward to a transformed Africa void of classism. I've come to a logical conclusion that classism has been the core reason why racism and terrorism exist, from our ideology of a people oriented government, recall that I have been propagating that as board members we must pursue a common objective and value void of classism, If we must succeed. Rwanda, Burundi, Sudan, Ethiopia, Sierra-Leon and many more have been broken and cracked down by the enemy called classism. We cannot continue this way. All men deserve equal rights; equality is a right when it comes to governance and policies as it affects the people. It is a huge crime to deprive some ethnic group in favor for the other; it is highly inhumane to favor a race than another. If we want to put an end to the trouble in this continent, one of the very root issues to tackle, to resolve and put a total end to is classism.

9

Africa and Racism

The term racism has always been the rival and color discrimination from the white against the black. Unfortunately, the traits and characteristics of racism have also crept into the black community. Racism was an idea originated by a certain class of race who believed in their delusional mind that they were more superior to others; this inhumane ideology gave birth to slave trade, colonization and every oppressive practices that ever existed in the history of mankind.

But this is the 21st century, and the whole world is almost civilized, and I believe that it is insane and delusional to think that the continent of Africa is a continent for the black

176

race only, considering our brothers from Northern Africa. Also naturalization by birth, migration in whatever form, refugees seeking asylum and of course, colonial implantation have made every part of the world a racial-mix. Today, there are black people who are not from Africa, and who don't even claim to be Africans, they may have had an African origin, but they are certainly not Africans.

It is imperative we discuss this underlying issue gradually cropping its way into the developing African society, I have heard blacks speak with so much hatred for the white or colored. I have heard black people say, they can't stand a white man. I have heard so much bitterness locked inside, I have seen so much hatred in display. People earn citizenship either by birth or as a result of living in a state or country for a period as deem the constitution to award citizenship.

We must all at this point begin to accept one another as one, and thus, begin to synergize our strengths to achieve more for this continent.

"Southern Africa is like a Zebra, you cannot remove the white or black from it and expect the Zebra to be alive."

Any politician seeking public supports with a claim or promise to send a particular race out of a country is simply day dreaming, I particularly address the Southern Africans of this great continent, we must all see the great side of the past, how it has made our countries the best in the continent. Nelson Mandela saw ahead what Robert Mugabe couldn't see. The younger generation of Africa today may not be fully aware neither would they grasp fully the negative impact or danger of racism.

If there is one thing I can attest to, it is the fact that racial discrimination has downgraded and trampled upon the confidence of the community who has suffered from it. The effect of racism is that it suddenly turns other people's opinion about you to almost become your reality, but I learned one thing listening to Les Brown, which was a statement made by the man who helped him see his own life from a completely new perspective, which is *"never let another man's opinion of you become your reality"*

Nonetheless, I strongly believe that the past must be left in the past, because to achieve your destiny you must crawl out of your past.

This chapter mainly focuses on the danger of reawakening racial discrimination through political policies and forums that are unhealthy to the growth of the envisioned continent, and who in today's Africa is the racist? However, before I begin unraveling my perspective to racism as it relates to the Africa of today, I consider of great necessity that we understand the true meaning of racism.

Racism is the greatest tragedy inflicted upon mankind by fellow mankind. Similar to classism, racism is more tuned to racial discrimination, and this was and has been the biggest battle between races. Some races believe they are superior and the most important race and so all rights must be

179

reserved for them. Decades ago, racism used to be a war between white and black. Mostly in the traditional American days, after the slave era, the blacks were supposedly freed, but the freedom was still with restrictions and discrimination, the white had more privilege than the former slave, this is what racism meant in those days. In the cause of my research I stumbled upon an article on www.about.com written by **Nadra KareemNittle** *Race Relations http://racerelations.about.com/od/understandingrac1/a/WhatIsRacism.htm*

I found something more profound and I felt it was of great importance to share with you the perspective and definition of this author.

"Today, the word racism is thrown around all the time by not only members of racial minority groups but by whites too. Use of the term "racism" has become so popular that it's spun off related terms such as "reverse racism," "horizontal racism" and "internalized racism."

Firstly, *racism is, "The belief that race accounts for differences in human character or ability and that a particular race is superior to others."*

Secondly, *racism is, "Discrimination or prejudice based on race."* Examples of the first definition abound. When slavery was practiced in the United States, blacks were not only considered inferior to whites but also regarded as property instead of human beings. During the 1787 Philadelphia Convention, it was agreed that slaves were to be considered three-fifths people for purposes of taxation and representation. Generally, during slavery, blacks were deemed intellectually inferior to whites. This notion persists in modern-day America.

Sadly, racism in the form of discrimination does exist in our society also. Africa in itself has suffered from racial discrimination of diverse measures, and we may want to attribute the flux of Africa's development and leadership on the fact that we have been tagged inferior. However, in time past, policies and constitutions may have supported the regime of dictatorial racist in government, but not in this age and time in Africa. Interestingly, Africa of today, especially countries where other races are in existence, still sees some level or low key racism in play. My first concern is to let you know, the continent Africa is not only a continent of the black. We may have more blacks, but Africa is not a 100% black continent. I personally believe, everybody is a migrant, you will agree with me that citizenship is earned by birth or by naturalization, so be you black, white, Asian, Dutch, Arab etc.

If you were born here or you have lived in any part of this continent for more than ten years, welcome home, for this is your home. I'm taking time to break this ice because this is where the root cause of discrimination lies, when some people suddenly believe they are more important than others or some believe the land is more theirs than others, then we are going to have a bit of a situation. Interestingly, today, blacks are also exhibiting the traits of racism in their dealing with other race in Africa, even against fellow black, there are internal wars going on, on this premises I can tell that racism as in its own way has gotten a hold of our politics in Africa. In so many Africa countries today, some tribes believe the seat of power is their inheritance, and that they are the best man fit for the position of ruler-ship than any other tribe. Like in my country Nigeria, relatively the northern Nigerians believe presidency is their birthright, and when they are not in power, then peace is withdrawn from the nation. Believe it or not, this is a form of racism.

Horizontal Racism

Horizontal racism? When this occurs, members of minority groups adopt racist attitudes towards other minority groups. An example of this would be if a Japanese American prejudged a Mexican American based on the racist stereotypes of Latinos found in mainstream culture.

Narrowing this to Africa, let me take South Africa as my case study. A rainbow nation as it is popularly called, with four races, the predominantly black who make up about

79.2% of the population. The white, which makes up about 8.9%, the Coloured which makes up 8.9% the Asian or Indian who makes up about 2.5% and others 0.5%, it is sometimes possible to see the Dutch discriminating the Asian, or even the white against the Dutch, this is horizontal discrimination, which is not needed if we really want to co-exist and grow together. The thought that one tribe, race or clan is more superior to the other is first a complete act of dehumanization, deprivation and discrimination, and when we now carry this mental greed into our politics, we are already breaking the foundation of unity and progress in our society.

If our foundations and core basis for coming together to form a nation were right, I believe we will not be fighting these wars, and if at this age and time, some group, tribe, race or sect still believes they are more superior to the other, then it is clear, we were never meant to be together. If we believe we are one people, one nation, with one hope and one dream, then the pride and glory should be first to uphold the honor and glory of our nations. The USA taught me one great lesson and how they as a people have broken the barriers of racial or tribal discrimination from their politics. Today a black man is the world most powerful man in the white house. That man is Barrack Obama, from a Kenyan Father, and during America's election, I had never seen or come across the flag of the Democrat neither have I seen that of the Republican Party.

What I see in every party campaign is the flag of the United States of America. This act shows that these people are of one belief, one dream, one country, and common core value. It is very much possible to overcome and say no to internalized and horizontal racism, we must begin to see ourselves as one people, one hope, one nation and one continent.

10

Africa and Terrorism

Terrorism is the greatest predicament the world has to combat today. Just like racism, terrorism is also an idea of prejudice hiding behind religion. Years ago, terrorism wasn't as profound as it has become today in Africa. It has become fiercer, more destructive, more deadly and more terrifying. Beliefs and faith are personal and a thing of choice, but the new generation terrorist wants the whole world to live by their own beliefs and practices.

In Africa today, so many things may have contributed to the issue of terrorism. One major factor that has contributed to terrorism is the lack of enlightenment and the concept of superiority, which in itself has been the breeding ground for terrorism. The superiority factor cuts across ethnicity and religion, these two differentiations are the root cause for terrorism thriving in Africa today. Terrorism is the unofficial or unauthorized use of violence and intimidation in the pursuit of political aims. Therefore, terrorists hide under the cloak of religion to instigate violence. It is mostly politically driven, the main objective of every terrorist is to seize power and control governments.

Terrorism is not new, and even though it has been used since the beginning of recorded history, it can be relatively hard to define. Terrorism has been described variously as both a tactic and strategy; a crime and a holy duty; a justified reaction to oppression and an inexcusable abomination. Obviously, a lot depends on whose point of view is being represented. Terrorism has often been an effective tactic for the weaker side in a conflict. Terrorism has become increasingly common among those pursuing extreme goals throughout the world, especially under developed continents such as Africa, Asia etc. However, despite its popularity, terrorism can be an indefinable concept. Even within the U.S. Government, agencies responsible for different functions in the ongoing fight against terrorism use different definitions.

The United States Department of Defense defines terrorism as *"the calculated use of unlawful violence or threat of unlawful violence to inculcate fear; intended to coerce or to intimidate governments or societies in the pursuit of goals that are generally political, religious, or ideological."* Within this definition, we can identify three key elements—violence, fear, and intimidation—and each element produce terror in its victims.

Terrorism is the unlawful use of force and violence against persons or property to intimidate or coerce a government, the civilian population, or any segment thereof, in furtherance of political or social objectives. The U.S. Department of State defines terrorism to be *"premeditated politically-motivated violence perpetrated against non-combatant targets by sub-national groups or clandestine agents, usually intended to influence an-audience".*

The strategy of terrorists is to commit acts of violence that draws the attention of the local populace, the government, and the world to their cause. The terrorists plan their attack to obtain the greatest publicity, choosing targets that symbolize what they oppose. The effectiveness of the terrorist act lies not in the act itself, but in the public or government's reaction to the act.

One third of the nations in Africa are under strong holds of various terrorist groups, and their singular objective is to seize political power and get government's attention, whatever the case may be. Ethnic rivalry or Religious rivalry, terrorism in itself is a big setback for development, for those who employ terrorism as a measure to enforce change by act of violence are only digging bottomless pits of trouble for the next generation.

How Terrorism Thrives

The untamed and unattended demands of some ethnic groups by the government has in its own way created a loop hole for terrorism to thrive in so many nations in Africa. For instance, in Nigeria, the youth of the rich oil region Niger-Delta decided to take laws into their hands, by kidnapping expatriates and destruction of oil pipelines of multinational companies in the region.

All was for them to gain public attention, and somehow it worked, because that got the government to pay attention to their demand. Boko Haram, ISIS, and any other terrorist group operating within Africa all have a demand, and the majority want political power, so when this attention is not attended to, the outburst escalates into what we know as terrorism.

African politics is centered on ethnicity, and our constitution has also approved the divide and rule policy, which in itself is the greatest support for ethnic discrimination. Take a deep look into your country and analyze the root causes for all violence or outburst since inception. You will frankly agree that it's all about ethnic superiority or marginalization. Poor distribution of wealth has also sparked conflict in Nigeria's oil-rich southern region, where militants lobbying for a greater share of oil revenue regularly blow up pipelines and kidnap foreign oil workers.

Andrew Kakabadse, Professor of International Management Development at the U.K.-based Cranfield School of Management, says oil companies have at various times pitted ethnic factions against one another for economic gain. Kakabadse blames a lethal combination of outside oil interests, long-standing local conflicts and poverty for the sectarian strife.

"In Nigeria the Christian-Muslim thing is the tip of the iceberg," he says. "What's underneath the water is a much more complex sociopolitical situation, which cannot be explained just in terms of the religious divide. You have a recipe ripe for conflict, and it just so happens to be Christian-Muslim."

191

Sectarian conflict erupted most profoundly in 1967, when three primarily Igbo eastern states seceded under the name Republic of Biafra, sparked a bloody three-year civil war. The attempt to break away ultimately failed, and Nigeria reintegrated the Igbo majority region in 1970.

However since this insurgence, the north has leveraged on it to seize power. They do not believe any other tribe or ethnic group has a right to the throne of the republic except them, and this is yet another fuel for trouble looming around. The other ethnic groups have also woken up to the fact that Nigeria is also theirs as it is to the north, and so every ethnic group or tribe now believes the best man for the job must come from their own tribe or ethnicity.

I have spoken more about Nigeria because it is my country and I have more information on my country than I do for others in Africa, but research has proven that the biggest railway for terrorism is ethnicity indifferences and religious intolerance. This is certainly not the kind of Africa we want to build for the next generation, because sooner or later, as it

192

has already began in Nigeria, the younger generation are already beginning to fault and curse the generations of the fathers who had the opportunity to make a difference but didn't. My generation has never seized from abusing and cursing the older generations and leaders who drove the nation into the pit it is. The reverse is the case, the average American child blesses the generation of the founding fathers of America, and the lives of these men and women have become the fountain and a source of inspiration for the average American youth.

As I have always iterated, we can seize the day and make a difference. Terrorism in Africa will be a thing of the past when we do what is necessary, when we break every barriers and prejudice or discrimination amongst ourselves. If the founding fathers of our nations lacked foresight, we can begin a new nation with a transformed thinking and enlightened generation who proffer solutions for change rather than complaining about or violently enforcing what will never be.

193

In relationships, we first find a common ground and reason why we want to be together and then we must always find a reason to stay together. Nigeria may not be physically heading for destruction or doom, but internally, we are a cracked and multi-divided generation.

How do this generation tackle the challenges of deprivation, discrimination, prejudice and massacre? Some school of thought including mine, has some time advocated we all go our separate ways.

Read more: *Nigeria Massacre: Violence Over Religion, Poverty in Jos.*
TIME http://content.time.com/time/world/article/0,8599,1971010,00.html#ixzz 2m2qgiwiS

So, it is high time we find a common ground and fair ground to play and live as one nation, one people with one purpose. This applies for your country as well. I live in South Africa today and what I see is a case of racial vendetta especially the black trying to fight back and punish the white for the evil and atrocities and deprivation they as black went through in the eras of apartheid.

Africa has come to the age of enlightenment and we must all pursue a common goal and objective, by which no measure or prejudice, classism, racism and terrorism will ever penetrate. A school of thought may believe it is never possible to change and become the envy of the world and the best continent on planet earth. Another school of thought may subscribe to the policy of violence, but the very minute few who believe change is possible, that in ten years, Africa will rule the world in all spheres and become the center focus for civilization in the next twenty years, these few elect are the ones I have written this book for.

Read and run with a vision for change, read and begin the change we desire to see. Read and enlighten others, as you are enlightened. We can no longer accept the positions and self-inflicted circumstances our visionless and unproductive leadership has conveyed upon us. We can make a difference and making a difference or pursuit for success is a deliberate action, not just mere wishful thinking. I'm speaking for my generation. I'm an illuminator; I'm a light to this continent, and to my generation, born to unravel the darkened wall of ignorance and mediocrity looming around our society. Though my arguments may not be completely true as it has not be ascertained and proven, but I have a feeling that my generation is the most migrated generation to western world since the beginning of time.

Gone are the days when people traveled from one location to the other for the pleasure of traveling or touring the world. My generation is in search of home as our so-called own country no longer befits home, as we have become strangers and voiceless in our own homelands, as we have been deprived of our rights and benefits from been a citizen or native of the land. We have chosen to run for our dear lives, millions of youths migrating from one nation or continents to the other, from Africa to Europe, are not only seeking greener pasture, rather in pursuit or in search for survival. But for how long shall we continue to run?

11

My African Dream

Now is the time to lift our nation from the quick sand of classism, racial injustice and terrorism to the solid rock of brotherhood.

Dr. Martin Luther King Jnr.

My African dream is simply my perspective and version of a new continent, with a generation of people renewed in their thinking, a people completely transformed through enlightenment and also equipped with noble character, a people willing to lay down best moral, spiritual and ethical principles that will govern the states and help prepare the foundation of development for the coming generation in all spheres of life. My African

197

dream is to behold a people bound by one purpose, one dream, one voice, and one hope. A people who seeks for the advancement of others than self, a continent void of classism, racism and terrorism, a continent where love, tolerance and mutual respect are the foundation and pillars holding our diversities together.

My African dream is to behold the nations of Africa practice true and people oriented democracy, where choice of leaders are not based on ethnicity, class or race, but are based on the competence, character and pedigree of the leadership and administrative acumen of each aspirants.

My African dream is to behold the nations of Africa void of hypocritical and deceitful politicians who lack ideas, plans and strategy, but go around sharing money and food when it's election time, all to manipulate the uneducated, poor and needy. My African dream is to behold Africa emerging as one of the top continents where education is at its best, matching global standard. I believe it is possible to become the continent with the best universities in the world.

My African dream is to behold the nations of Africa being managed and nurtured as a trans-generational business entity geared towards making profits by first providing the best service and producing quality products capable of generating the expected profits.

My African dream is to wake up one day and behold all the nations in this continent have great visionary leaders as presidents and public service officers who are purpose driven, selfless, and dreamers who will do all within to see their dream come true for the people and the nation.

My African dream is to behold a continent where violence will never prevail anymore, where the love that abounds amidst the people will help create an amicable and peaceful way to resolve misunderstanding rather than choosing war, we will choose peace and unity.

My African dream is to behold a continent where elections are based on true democratic process and not rigging as the case has always been.

I see transformed nations of Africa.

I see a purpose driven people passionately pursuing the remolding and rebuilding of the foundations of our nations.

In conclusion, dreams are pictures of a preferred future, painted in our imaginations, and can only become a reality when we act on them.

I have begun my own path to making my African dream a reality. I will voice out as much as I can. I will provide platforms to enlighten, educate and empower my generation and the next on what I believe must be done to see Africa transformed.

Will you fold your hands and complain as we've always done?

Or

Will you join the bandwagon to destroy the country and continent further?

Or

Will you sit there, detached and do nothing?

Or

Will you become the voice of change; acting out your dream to make your country and this continent what it is originally designed to be.

You Decide...

Love, Gratitude, and Forgiveness

12

Love is a purpose of human life, no matter who is controlling it, it is to love whoever is around to be loved.

Tonito Samuel

I believe the deterioration and rot in Africa today can only be healed through a supernatural process. The introduction of Christianity and other peace driven religions and their practices have taught a great deal of human behavior and people management to a large extent. The teaching I learned from the book of the law of the Christian faith has proven to me that there are applicable and generally acceptable standards of how man can coexist in love and appreciation of fellow men.

I do not imply other religions have not dealt with the subject matter as well. I can boldly say that virtually all religion practiced in Africa today has something to talk about love, gratitude and forgiveness, and this chapter is focused on how these three natures and mindset can transform and reform this continent. The conflicts and misappropriations in Africa have caused a lot of damage that can only be revived through a process, and for this process not to be aborted, we need to understand that we must lay a better and refined foundation for our nation and our people.

In so doing we must accept that the healing we seek lies in love, gratitude and forgiveness. These were the secrets of the icon and father of Africa, Nelson Mandela. These are the very first teachings Jesus Christ taught the people while he talked about the beatitude. From the teaching of Jesus Christ, it was clear that you cannot claim to love your neighbor when the love is not measured with the kind of love you give to yourself.

203

"Love is what makes us god, because God is love, and the only way we become like HIM is when we love,"

"Love has nothing to do with what you are expecting to get — only with what you are expecting to give — which is everything."

"To love is the greatest sacrifice, because it compels and coerces you to accept people for who they are and learn to live happily with them even when they hurt you, you to find a better way to correct them because you love them."

Only a fool and a wicked person will continue to hurt you even when you keep loving them.

"Love is a purpose of human life, no matter who is controlling it, it is to love whoever is around to be loved.

"What is love but acceptance of the other, whoever he is.

"Love looks not with the eyes, but with the mind.

Love is the greatest weapon of warfare, for it fights not to hurt, but to heal, not to win but to warm, love is selfless, and love is the greatest sacrifice on earth.

Love is what we need to cure, heal and put behind the past

and restart a destiny of a new refined and reformed continent called Africa. Love is what makes everybody equal, irrespective of our culture, color, class or credo. Love is the healing the world needs, for love knows no boundaries, love knows no hate, love keeps no record of evil, love does not discriminate, love does not count itself to be better or preferred to another, love is giving, love is forbearing, love is tolerance, love is righteousness. Love is the greatest secret great men who have left landmark impacts on planet earth gave to humanity that makes them iconic.

For example, Nelson Mandela, of blessed memory, only embraced love, and gave love back to those who were his oppressors and prosecutors and that singular mindset, was the game changer for him, his family, South Africa, Africa and the world at large. Love is of course a word that comes and goes around, but if only people knew what love really is? The world will be a better place to live in, for love is the foundation for change, newness, progress and prosperity.

Love is the greatest gift to mankind, and because we have been given the grace and nature to love, we can make a huge difference. One of my greatest songs of all time is One Love, keep us together, by Bob Marley, because love breeds unity, unity breed greater accomplishment and achievements. *A bible passage says, one will chase a thousand and two will chase ten thousand.*

I want to urge you to begin from this day to spring forth love wherever you are. The world needs you, I need you, and you sure do need me. We all need each other to survive, and love is the only secret that will bind us together as cord that cannot be broken.

Learn to love. Learn to treat people as much as you love to be treated. Love will teach you how to respect people's choices and opinion and when they appear wrong before you. Love will teach you how to find a better way to help them see their wrongs, not by judgment, but by love, you can drive folly far away from the human mind. While growing up, from my father, I learned that life is the greatest teacher and not experience alone, and that the lesson to learn from life is 'Love'. Do you love your country? If you truly do, then don't allow it to be ruined and destroyed by evil men and women who are after nothing but their selfish ambitions. Fight for it, stand for it, let love rule over you and you will see the difference between love and hate.

Forgiveness

- The concept of forgiveness is such an interesting issue to discuss and share with people anytime any day, why? Because, beyond the paroxysms, it goes deeper to affect our emotion and psychology, if we allow the absence of forgiveness to permeate. It breeds resentments, resentments breeds hatred and hatred is the destroyer of peace and unity in any society.

- We cannot discuss moving forward for a better continent without first addressing forgiveness, because of the resultant effect of the lack of vision and purpose. The effects of classism and prejudice have left many hearts broken and minds hurt. We must begin by openly and deep within our hearts, souls and bodies forgive and forget.

- This was Nelson Mandela's principle, a strategy that not only healed the land, but also, freed the prisoner and the jailer all at the same time for a life of peace and unity. I am a church boy and I have been taught countless times what forgiveness is, and in my research, I stumbled into a deeper perspective of forgiveness by a psychologist, Sonja Lyubomirsky

What is forgiveness?

Psychologist Sonja Lyubomirsky calls forgiveness "a shift in thinking" towards someone who has wronged you, "such that your desire to harm that person has decreased and your desire to do him good (or to benefit your relationship) has increased." Forgiveness, at a minimum, is a decision to let go of the desire for revenge and ill will toward the person who wronged you.

Forgiveness is something that is entirely up to you. Although reconciliation may follow forgiveness, it is possible to forgive without re-establishing or continuing the relationship. The person you forgive may be deceased or no longer part of your life. You may also choose not to reconcile, perhaps because you have no reason to believe that a relationship with the other person is healthy for you.

Forgiveness is not condoning or excusing. Forgiveness does not minimize, justify, or excuse the wrong that was done. Forgiveness also does not mean denying the harm and the feelings of hurt. We grew up to learn the saying that; *To err is human and to forgive is divine*. The ability to forgive and forget the hurts and press forward shows you have a large heart, if you can love, you can forgive.

This dimension of forgiveness may sound a little too extreme or religious for some people to comprehend, but if there is anything we must agree on, it is the fact that forgiveness has higher benefits than we can possibly imagine, just to mention a few, below is the lists of benefits.

Benefits of forgiveness

There are three typical responses to being wronged: reciprocating with equal harm, avoiding the person, or seeking revenge. Forgiveness, on the other hand, is a conscious decision to offer generosity and mercy that a person's actions do not deserve. And, paradoxically, by forgiving another, we benefit ourselves.

The growing body of research on forgiveness is finding that people who forgive are more likely than the general population to have:

- Fewer episodes of depression
- Higher self-esteem
- More friends
- Longer marriages
- Lower blood pressure
- Closer relationships

- Fewer stress-related health issues
- Better immune system function
- Lower rates of heart disease

And they are more likely to be happy, serene, empathetic, hopeful, and very much more agreeable people.

Sources: *The How of Happiness*, by Sonja Lyubomirsky *Learning to Forgive May Improve Well-Being*, Mayo Clinic

As a child in the Sunday school, I thought forgiveness was a religious and spiritual experience and that it was only a principle taught in the Christian faith. As I grew older and knew better, I discovered all of the major faith traditions include forgiveness as a central value. However, forgiveness is so universal to our human experience that it plays a large role across faith traditions as well as among people who do not practice a religion. Because forgiveness is first an emotional healing that transcends to our emotions, and in turn defines how we react to the parties who may have caused the hurts and unfortunately how we react to our environment.

Gratitude

To be thankful, appreciative and content with your life is yet another great principle and tool for prosperity in any society. The last one year of my life, I have developed a culture to write down each day what I am grateful for, and I have seen tremendous progress in my entire life. Gratitude is first, self-acceptance and self-contentment, and for the Africa of today, this is far becoming an imaginary culture that may never be realized.

As the tough conditions of living dwindles, economic circumstances does not seem to give anybody any reason to want to be grateful for being an African, with exception of our neighbors from Southern African region. I have come to understand from life experiences that what you appreciate, appreciates, and what you are grateful for becomes graceful and receives the potential to grow. The essence of this topic is to create an aggressive consciousness and an awakening in the life of our youths, that, it is not time to give up yet, and neither will there ever be any reason to throw in the towel. If we play our roles effectively, it is not time to back off nor is it time to get done with it as the slangs is today, but rather a time to reflect on the essence why the creator had made it possible that we had to come from the country we all came from and grab the grace of gratitude and ask deeper questions such as why have I been born to this country and of what purpose am I here to fulfill?

Afterwards find purpose and pursue it with all tenacity. Growing up, my mother would always make this statement when we complained about life and situations, *"Nobody chooses where he comes from, nor chooses who his parents would be, but God"*. That is forever a very profound statement of truth. That if only we can think of the good and greatness that lies within our country and be grateful to God for

213

making us a part of a nation, and seeing beyond the plagues and turmoil's of injustice and prejudice, to visualize a dream country where love, justice, peace reigns, we will begin to feel proud and responsible to make a difference in our country.

Trust me, I can affirmatively say to you that Nigeria has not done enough for me and my generation, a great leader once said to Americans, *Stop thinking of what America will do for you, but think of what you can do for America,* I think that statement can also be directed to us in Africa.

Especially Nigerian youths and so many countries in Africa, to be called a Nigerian today seem like a curse. When we appear in any part of the world, it's like evil, danger and the devil has just appeared. Even with our very entrepreneurial mindset, the negative about us is still higher than the good we display. The pride to be associated with the country is gone. If it were possible to exchange the green passport in the supermarket, 75% would do it without a blink. The days when Nigeria was the giant of Africa are long gone, and we are living in the shadows of our past glory. I have actually concluded, Nigeria's biggest tragedy is the blessing that has become a curse.

Nonetheless, I believe Nigeria will rise again. I feel very much grateful for being a Nigerian, and that I can be the channel of reformation for my country and Africa, for this cause I will assume a more responsible role and switch for the shift, embrace the change and run with a vision for a greater Africa.

Let us become a people with a heart of gratitude, so that the universe will shower on us the blessing for gratitude and grace our lands with blessings of responsible leadership, purpose driven men and women, whose vision reaches out to all without prejudice.

Thank You!

Appreciation

Firstly, my appreciation goes to the great men and leaders who inspired my thinking and principles. My warm appreciations go to *Tata Nelson Rolihlahla Mandela* of blessed memory, in whose legacy I ride on to share and discuss my dream for a new Africa, and for every great leader this continent has produced in various tiers. Also, my thanks goes to those whose leadership paradigms have helped me become better. I celebrate Rev. Sam Adeyemi, whose teachings and messages has been my greatest motivations and to so many of you who have influenced my life that time will not permit me to begin to mention.

To my lovely wife Lydia and daughter Mozare, you guys have been my most understanding buddies, to Oluwaseun Kolawole, for the concepts and advice on making this book a reality, I say big thank you. To Dare-Noble Oluwasanmi for all your contribution to the success of this book, I say thank you and to all my friends whom I have engaged in many impromptu discussion just to catch a different perspective of some issues as regarding the state of Africa, I sincerely want to thank you. In addition, to the many who have played a vital role in the making of this book! You guys Rock! And I say a big **Thank you!**

About The Author

___

Tonito Samuel, *CEO 1VA Technologies (Pty) Ltd*. A self-motivated, purpose driven and creative visionary, and multi-talented individual with great business development skills; A computer science graduate from Lagos State University, a software architect, a web entrepreneur, a strategist, a public speaker and a life coach. He is the founder of 1voice Africa, an African oriented social networking platform, which is emerging as the biggest information platform in Africa today. http://www.1voiceafrica.com, He is also the Principal Consultant at The Mind Coach Academy. Author of the book "2030, This Time of Your Life. A book positioning the 20's and 30's generation on the importance of effective use of timing. Tonito is very resourceful, goal oriented and tenacious. He is someone who stops at nothing until his ideas materialize, never settles at his achievements. He is always pressing on for greater heights and accomplishments. Visit www.tonitosamuel.co.za for more

About 1voice Africa

1Voice Africa is Africa's number one social network platform that provides an ambience for friends to connect, interact, learn and lead the transformation and repositioning bound to take place. We bridge the gap between Africa and the world. We firmly believe it's time to showcase the rich culture and trends that make Africa unique. Join Africa's largest online community today and **Enjoy Africa!**

For more information, visit

https://www.1voiceafrica.com/about

About MIC

Recent research has shown a high level of irresponsibility's amidst the youths of this generation, who have chosen a pattern to engage with extreme pleasure rather than pursue a life of purpose. We've only got one life, and wisdom teaches us to make it count, rather than recklessly wasting our lives on pleasures that drives us to the edges of destruction. It became my prerogative and my mission to help young people struggling with drugs and defect of social vices affecting their progress in life. Hence. MIC was born.

MIC is an acronym for Make-It-Count, an initiative put together to inspire the youths of this generation to dream.

In order to be effective, a cause had to be born, a cause aimed at recording a high positive societal impact and life transforming moments for the youths of Africa. Crime and Drug Free Africa (CADFA) became the product of this

221

collective project, because we believe it is one major area the government, religious bodies and non profit making organizations will want to see change for good in our societies.

Our Mission

To build a crime and drug free society in Africa, by this mandate, we will pursue a life counseling programs aimed at eradicating or reducing Crime rate to its barest minimum and completely rid the society of drug, with strategic informative programs designed to help the youths Discover, Develop and Deploy the greatness inside.

Join Our Cause Today!
1voiceafrica.com/cadfa

About TMC

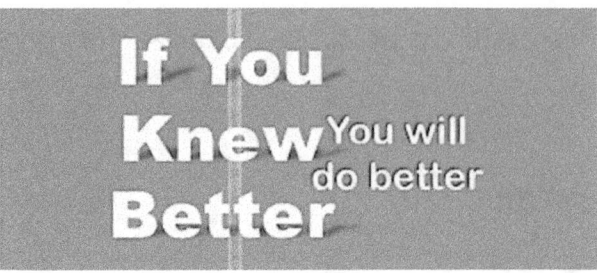

One can only function to the capacity he has developed the mind. And that's why champions have coaches… Who is coaching you?

Contact

Personal-Development – Corporate-Training – Career - Assessments – Talent-Hunting & Teen - Grooming,

For more information visit

www.tmcacademy.co.za

223

Register For Our Online Courses Today!

Course Title	Course Description	Duration:
3-Dimensions of Life	This is a foundational course essentially for all who desire to be the best in life. Objective: Help participants discover, develop and deploy their God given potential to the fullest.	**14 days.**
Creative Positive Thinking	This is a basic mind development process course essential for building a progressive lifestyle . Objective: Help participants develop a positive thinking and creative pattern of living.	**21 days.**
Strategic Repositioning	This is an advanced development course essential for building a progressive lifestyle. Objective: Help participants find the right place where they function best in the sphere of life.	**14 days.**
Anatomy of Relationship	This is a foundational course essential for those who desire to	**14 days.**

	win and win with people. Objective: Help participants find the meaning and benefit of relationship and people in life.	
Effective Leadership	This is a program for those who desire to learn the act of effective and progressive leadership. Objective: Help participants develop the leader inside	**14 days.**
Spirituality, Love & Gratitude	This is a FREE course designed for those who desire understanding of Spirituality, Love and Gratitude. Objective: Help participants find deep understanding of Spirituality, Love & Gratitude in the sphere of life.	**3 Days**

For enquiries visit

www.tmcademy.co.za

Other books by Tonito Samuel.....

■

■

226